Faith and History
Essays on Prayer, Exile, and Return

מגיד
MAGGID

Rabbi Eliezer Berkovits

Faith and History

Essays on Prayer, Exile, and Return

EDITED BY

Zev Eleff

Maggid Books

Faith and History
Essays on Prayer, Exile, and Return

Maggid Books
An imprint of Koren Publishers Jerusalem Ltd.

POB 8531, New Milford, CT 06776-8531, USA
& POB 4044, Jerusalem 9104001, Israel
www.korenpub.com

The publication of this book was made possible through the generous support of *The Jewish Book Trust.*

ISBN 978-1-59264-641-8, *hardcover*

Printed and bound in the United States

In loving memory of

RABBI ELIEZER AND MRS. SALI BERKOVITS, *z"l*

We are eternally grateful for their many years of guidance and friendship. We are confident that the publication of Faith and History: Essays on Prayer, Exile, and Return *will inspire a new generation as they inspired us.*

Howard N. z"l and Jacqueline Gilbert
Stephen J. and Elizabeth Landes
Jack and Ana Berger

In loving memory of

HOWARD N. GILBERT, *z"l*

devoted student of the Rabbi,
outstanding attorney and counselor,
life-long learner, creative philanthropist, and loyal friend.
He is greatly missed.

Contents

SECTION 3: RETURN

Introduction

In July 1950, Congregation Adath Jeshurun of Roxbury called Rabbi Dr. Eliezer Berkovits to its pulpit. The Jews of the so-called Blue Hill Avenue Synagogue in the Boston neighborhood were eager to welcome the forty-one-year-old, Romanian-born, German-trained scholar. Since 1906, worshippers at the Blue Hill Avenue Synagogue had prayed in "probably the finest structure of its kind in New England."[1] The founders were a small wealthy group of modern-leaning Jews. Well before midcentury, those well-heeled congregants had moved on, resettling in more affluent Boston suburbs. They were replaced in Roxbury by a larger circle of devout, working-class Jews at Adath Jeshurun. This second iteration practiced a more traditional form of Judaism but also appreciated modern scholarship and culture.[2] They also held deep convictions and commitment to the Zionist cause. Their views comported with the Orthodox Jews that Berkovits had previously led in Germany,

1. Gerald H. Gamm, "In Search of Suburbs: Boston's Jewish Districts," in *The Jews of Boston: Essays on the Occasion of the Centenary (1895–1995) of the Combined Jewish Philanthropies of Greater Boston* (Boston: Combined Jewish Philanthropies of Greater Boston, 1995), 144.
2. Ibid., 148.

England, and Australia. Eliezer Berkovits, then, was a very good match for this Boston-based congregation.

The Berkovitses – Eliezer, Sali, and their three sons – moved into a modest-sized, second-floor apartment on 8 Montana Street in September 1950.[3] In Boston, Berkovits told a journalist that he wished to "give traditional Judaism 'a modern Orthodox expression.'" This term, Modern Orthodoxy, was not yet in vogue but Berkovits must have anticipated its utility.[4] He was very impressed with Boston. He marveled at the neighborhood streetcars and the "modern trains" that pulled in and out of South Station and the "uniform good quality and hygienic preparation and handling of food obtainable, even at the railway station."[5] Owing to the progressive inclinations and technological prowess in the United States, Berkovits believed that his avant-garde academic credentials and philosophical background would suitably and ably "translate [Judaism] into the language of our times." Unlike him, most of Berkovits' congregants did not hold college degrees. But they understood his accessible sermonic stylings and told their college-bound children to pay attention to their rabbi's diction and directions.

Eliezer Berkovits took stock of his new surroundings. He delayed his start at the Blue Hill Avenue Synagogue by a few weeks so that he might study his flock, the "various phases of the Roxbury community." More open to cooperation among different streams of Judaism than other Orthodox elements, Berkovits "hope[d] to work with all positive Jewish forces" and desired to "influence those who have drifted away from active religious forms of life."[6] Most specifically, he hoped to reacquaint his coreligionists with the core values of prayer and negotiate the tension of Jewish life in the Diaspora and in Israel.

Rabbi Berkovits did not publish or preserve his sermons from his seven-year sojourn in Boston. However, newspaper articles from the

3. "Cong. Adath Jeshurun to Install Dr. Berkovits as Rabbi on Sunday," *Jewish Advocate*, February 8, 1951, 5.
4. See Zev Eleff, *Modern Orthodox Judaism: A Documentary History* (Lincoln, NE: University of Nebraska Press, 2016), 171–72.
5. "Roxbury Rabbi-Elect Saw Nazi Pogroms, London Blitz," *Jewish Advocate*, September 10, 1950, C37.
6. Ibid.

local Jewish press confirm that Berkovits carried through with his intentions. For instance, reports highlighted his lectures on Religious Zionism, the priorities of education, and the challenge of Jewish living in a modern society.[7] The descriptions of the University of Berlin–trained philosopher in this period paint him more like a sociologist, perhaps an anthropologist. In op-eds and popular-styled articles, some reproduced in these pages, Berkovits grappled with the fears of fast-paced technology and media. He worried about the chasms this caused between older Jewish immigrants and their modern children. He sympathized with his fellow Jews who found it difficult to find meaning in prayer amid political and social upheaval.[8]

Berkovits the communal leader did not emphasize metaphysics or other complex formulations of academic learning in his commentary. In these more "accessible" moments, Berkovits dwelled on the "human existence," something that he would have described as "philosophical anthropology," since it mainly drew on Jewish concepts and cultural tools rather than his considerable philosophical range.[9] To be sure, proof texts from the Torah, Talmud, and other canonical sources were also a major feature of Berkovits' writings. His philosophical writings, even the most technical and learned types, bring together the worlds of philosophy and Torah. His popular pieces are likewise anchored in Scripture; his sacred citations are reinforced by Berkovits' social observations and commonsense reasoning. But, in contrast to his academic works that placed Berkovits in dialogue with contemporary philosophers and scholars, his popular-styled output was addressed to his fellow Jews. A gifted writer, Berkovits expertly balanced erudite learning with accessible prose, even if, as I imagine, the exercise of withholding the copious footnoting he deployed in his other work sometimes pained him. Nonetheless, the utility of this approach was one of the few points at which Berkovits found

7. See, for example, Eliezer Berkovits, "Failure in Our Hebrew Schools?" *Jewish Advocate*, February 25, 1954, 15.
8. All these qualities are captured in Eliezer Berkovits, "Has God Bungled Creation?" *Jewish Advocate*, September 26, 1957, C1.
9. Eliezer Berkovits, *A Jewish Critique of the Philosophy of Martin Buber* (New York: Yeshiva University, 1962), 38.

agreement with Martin Buber; it was also shared by his contemporary and leading American Orthodox figure, Rabbi Joseph B. Soloveitchik.[10]

This had worked very well for Berkovits before his arrival in Boston: themes related to Zionism, Exile, and prayer abound in published versions of sermons he had delivered at the United Hebrew Congregation in Leeds, England.[11] If his Boston talks resembled the ones delivered in Britain, then they were certainly filled with biblical references and citations from the Talmud and Jewish medieval philosophers.

Berkovits left Boston in 1958 to serve as professor of philosophy at Hebrew Theological College (HTC). The school was in the process of relocating from Chicago's West Side to more suburban Skokie, and Berkovits was part of HTC leadership's plan to reenergize the entire institution.[12] To an alumnus, President Oscar Z. Fasman wrote that "I think I have one definite achievement in the educational field of the Yeshiva by having brought to the Faculty Dr. Eliezer Berkovits. He is an excellent man in the field of philosophy, he is genuinely pious, and what is very important from our point of view is the fact that he is a wonderful teacher who holds the interest of all the students in his class."[13]

That last point about Berkovits' reputation is, as Fasman relayed, "very important." Berkovits was not just a first-rate philosopher. He was a master educator and thought leader. In short order and in his new Chicago environs, Berkovits regained his footing as a public scholar and teacher. In this capacity, Orthodox Jews in Chicago seemed to appreciate him as much as his congregants back in Boston. The Religious Zionists of Chicago (Mizrachi) reminded its members that "Chicago Jewry is fortunate to have the services of such a scholar teaching at the Hebrew

10. Joseph B. Soloveitchik, *The Emergence of Ethical Man*, ed. Michael S. Berger (Jersey City, NJ: Ktav, 2005). See also Alex S. Ozar, "The Emergence of Max Scheler: Understanding Rabbi Joseph Soloveitchik's Philosophical Anthropology," *Harvard Theological Review* 109 (April 2016): 178–206.

11. E. Berkovits, *Between Yesterday and Tomorrow* (Oxford: The East and West Library, 1945).

12. See Oscar Z. Fasman, "After Fifty Years, an Optimist," *American Jewish History* 69 (December 1979): 167.

13. Oscar Z. Fasman to Uri Miller, May 28, 1958, Uri Miller File, Hebrew Theological College Archives, Skokie, IL.

Theological College."[14] In September 1969, Berkovits was one of the founders of the Skokie Orthodox Congregation, soon after renamed Congregation Or Torah. At Or Torah, Berkovits served as the "Ritual Chairman" (before the congregation hired a rabbi) and helped shepherd the young congregation.[15] Beyond Chicago, Berkovits was sought after to provide religious and social commentary. In 1966, the Council of Orthodox Jewish Congregations in Baltimore, Maryland, invited him to speak on "What Is the Jewish Tradition in Today's Movement for Civil Rights."[16] To an Orthodox leader in Minnesota, Fasman wrote of the great utility of Berkovits' writings on behalf of his tradition-bound faith community:

> Under separate cover I am sending you the best criticism that has ever been written on Reconstructionist thinking. The author is Dr. Berkovits, the head of our Philosophy department. The statement that it is the "best" is not mine alone, but is the declaration of a philosopher in the Reform movement, Rabbi Emil Fackenheim. You might want to keep this article with you, in case there are a few intellectuals in your audience who will raise some theoretical matters.[17]

Just as in Boston, Berkovits in his Midwestern climes embraced the chance to serve as a poignant spokesman of his faith and a public

14. "City-Wide Cultural Program," *Sabbath Voice* 25 (March 14, 1969): 1.
15. See, for example, Congregation Or Torah Minutes, Resolution on February 1970, Congregation Or Torah, Skokie, IL. In the board minutes, Berkovits took a very strong stance against a "certain individual who has not conducted himself in a manner befitting membership in or attendance at this Congregation." Berkovits "pointed out that halachically, if such an individual were to persist in attending services the members of the Congregation could and should ignore the individual, even to the point of not counting him for purposes of a Minyan."
16. "Old Business," in Meeting Minutes of the Council of Orthodox Jewish Congregations, October 10, 1966, Council of Orthodox Jewish Congregations, Box 1, MS-144, Jewish Museum of Maryland, Baltimore, MD.
17. Oscar Z. Fasman to Lewis N. Ginsberg, October 20, 1960, Lewis Ginsberg File, Hebrew Theological College Archives. Fasman was referencing Eliezer Berkovits, "Reconstructionist Theology: A Critical Evaluation," *Tradition* 2 (Fall 1959): 20–66.

educator. In like manner, Berkovits remained a courageous commentator on behalf of Orthodox Judaism and Religious Zionism in the final stretch of his career, upon settling in Israel in the 1970s.[18]

Descriptions of Eliezer Berkovits as an "anthropologist" and "social commentator" may come as a surprise. This part of Berkovits' oeuvre is different from his better-known philosophical treatises on ecumenism, theodicy, and the limits of change in Jewish law.[19] Both types demonstrated deep Torah learning. Yet, Berkovits' more familiar work was the stuff of rigorous philosophy. Many of these writings appeared later in Berkovits' career and, within some circles, marked him a "radical."[20]

It's not just Berkovits' later works that stand in contrast to his philosophical anthropology on prayer and modern life. Even before then, of all his work produced in the 1950s and 1960s, scholarly readers are best acquainted with Berkovits' erudite defense of Judaism against the charges of British historian Arnold Toynbee and his critical essays of Jewish philosophers Martin Buber, Hermann Cohen, Abraham Joshua Heschel, Mordecai Kaplan, and Franz Rosenzweig.[21] Embracing his role as a phalanx-like defender of Orthodox Judaism and undaunted critic of the non-Orthodox, Berkovits soon after collected these trenchant analyses into a book, for which he was unanimously awarded the 1975

18. See, for example, Eliezer Berkovits, "Like All the Nations?" *Jerusalem Post*, May 4, 1976, A29.
19. For one of the best assessments of Berkovits' thought, see Steven T. Katz, "Eliezer Berkovits and Modern Jewish Philosophy," *Tradition* 17 (Fall 1977): 92–138.
20. Shalom Carmy, "Eliezer Berkovits' Challenge to Contemporary Orthodoxy," *Torah u-Madda Journal* 12 (2004): 193. For some sources on Berkovits' so-called halakhic radicalism, see Chaim E. Twerski, "The Limiting Factors of Halacha: The Other Side of the Coin," *Academic Journal of Hebrew Theological College* 1 (November 2001): 80–106. See also Marc B. Shapiro, *Between the Yeshiva World and Modern Orthodoxy: The Life and Works of Rabbi Jehiel Jacob Weinberg, 1884–1966* (Oxford: Littman Library, 1999), 190–92.; and Gil Graff, "Halakhah as *Torat Hayyim*: The Values-Conscious Visions of Eliezer Berkovits and Emanuel Rackman," *Journal of Modern Jewish Studies* 18 (2019): 330–42. Also, Rahel Berkovits, "Torah *Hayyim*: The Status of Women in the Thought of Eliezer Berkovits," *Shofar* 31 (Summer 2013): 4–15.
21. For his critique of Toynbee, see Eliezer Berkovits, *Judaism: Fossil of Ferment?* (New York: Philosophical Library, 1956).

National Jewish Book Award's prize for Jewish thought.[22] Other learned readers, as David Hazony has pointed out, gained a firm appreciation of Berkovits' notion of moral philosophy through his pathbreaking tome, *God, Man and History*, published in 1959.[23]

Hazony's collection of Berkovits' "Essential Essays" captures the latter's philosophical energies, ranging from his views on Jewish law to post-Holocaust theology, Jewish morality, and Zionism. Hazony's volume remains an excellent resource; I trust that this book complements the "Essential Essays." In particular, the present volume reintroduces readers to the anthropological side of Eliezer Berkovits. Like all his work, Berkovits' Torah stands out as the marquee element of his thought. Torah was the primary material Berkovits wished to convey to his readers. But whereas the audience of his major philosophical works were fellow scholars, Berkovits wrote his philosophical anthropology for a smart but wider audience in mind. This, I believe, is borne out in the pages before you. This book's chapters are mostly drawn from the middle years of Berkovits' scholarly career: as a rabbinic leader in Leeds, Sydney, Boston, and then as a public intellectual in Skokie. Interested readers should review the bibliographical section of this volume for more detailed information.

This volume is arranged in three sections. The first engages Berkovits' thoughts on the synagogue and prayer. The first essay, "From the Temple to Synagogue and Back," blends history and rabbinic tradition to offer, ultimately, as Berkovits described it, a "psychological" critique of the postwar American Orthodox synagogue. The section's other chapters are drawn from a pamphlet Berkovits authored a few years later for Yeshiva University's "Studies in Torah Judaism" series. Berkovits, applauded by the series' editors, "fill[ed] an urgent need in our effort to establish a rationale of Torah Judaism."[24] Reviewers described Berkovits' psychological approach to prayer as "Heschelian," an ironic

22. Eugene B. Borowitz, "1975 National Jewish Book Awards of the JWB Jewish Book Council," *Jewish Book Annual* 33 (1975–1976): 267–68.
23. See David Hazony, "Introduction," in Eliezer Berkovits, *Essential Essays on Judaism*, ed. David Hazony (Jerusalem: Shalem Press, 2002), xxiv–xxv.
24. Sam Hartstein, "Publication of 2 New Studies in Our Series 'Studies in Torah Judaism'" press release, August 23, 1962, Yeshiva University Records, Public Relations People

description given Berkovits' scathing critique of Heschel that would appear two years later.[25] Nonetheless, the comparison rings true. Both Berkovits and Heschel stressed the role of prayer to help the worshipper become more "God-ward" or "God-centered." For Berkovits, and in keeping with his Holocaust theology, prayer ought to be used as a tool for human improvement and introspection rather than a chance to ask God to intercede.[26]

This volume's second and third sections, on Exile and Return, are, of course, interrelated. To be sure, these chapters do not represent Berkovits' most concrete statements on Zionism or the role of Zionists residing outside of Israel. This is probably best captured in the final chapter of his *Faith After the Holocaust*.[27] Instead, these chapters analyze how the notions of Eretz Yisrael and *galut* have affected Jewish living – for all Jews. Along these lines, Berkovits was concerned with how the unprecedented political freedoms accorded to Jews in the United States seemingly released them from maintaining connections with their Jewish identities and with Israel. Even worse, to Berkovits, was the effect of modern media and technology, and their confluence with American consumer culture. "The traditional or historic forms of Jewish living have been caught in a process," worried Berkovits, "of continually advancing disorganization, and the vacuum thus created has been invaded by living practices based on the one-day wisdom of newspapers and magazines,

Collection. Box 117, Folder: Stitskin, Leon, Yeshiva University Archives, New York, NY.

25. Chaim Feuerman, "Review of *Kaddish* and *Prayer*," *Tradition* 7 (Winter 1964–1965): 126. For Berkovits' criticism of Heschel, see Eliezer Berkovits, "Dr. A. J. Heschel's Theology of Pathos," *Tradition* 6 (Spring–Summer 1964): 67–104. While Berkovits' critical essays (mentioned above) seem to always carry with them severe tones, his review of Heschel was particularly sharp. See Todd Berman, "Berkovits, Heschel, and Heresy of Divine Pathos," *Tradition* 54 (Fall 2022): 50–90; and Shai Held, *Abraham Joshua Heschel: The Call of Transcendence* (Bloomington: Indiana University Press, 2013), 156–57.

26. On Berkovits' Holocaust theology, see Zev Eleff, "The Content and Context of Rabbi Eliezer Berkovits' Faith," in Eliezer Berkovits, *Faith After the Holocaust* (New Milford, CT: Maggid Books, 2019), 175–90; and David Hazony, "The Man Who Saved God from the Holocaust," *Shofar* 31 (Summer 2013): 54–73.

27. Berkovits, *Faith After the Holocaust*, 147–61.

on mass-produced thinking and streamlined feeling, on the standards of taste of the motion picture industry and the values of the TV screen."[28]

Here and elsewhere, Berkovits believed that the antidote would come, owing to his efforts at HTC and fealty toward Yeshiva University, in the training of Modern Orthodox rabbis.[29] These well-attuned rabbinic leaders, hoped Berkovits, could reconnect the intergenerational divide of an older European-born generation that felt the urgency of Jewish living and Zionism, and a young, American-raised generation that lacked the experiences and resolve to activate their religious identities. Without the old guard, he feared, American Jews lacked the substantive models to move forward, particularly in their connections with the "secular" elements within the State of Israel:

> In the present situation, its premises – when applied to the American scene – do not point to the road to Zion. And all talk about Zionist education and cultural links with the Jewish State, about Jewish pride and self-interest, will not induce American Jewry to seek its redemption in Israel. It will support Israel; it will take genuine pride in the achievements of the Jewish State and rightly so; it will well appreciate its self-interest in the state's security and well-being; it will send visitors as well as money to Israel; it will even organize Hebrew classes; yet America will still be no *galut*. The paradoxical situation has arisen that in the phase of Zionism's triumph, its reason for the rejection of the *galut* have conditioned hosts of good Zionists to reject the idea of *geula* in Zion for themselves.[30]

28. Eliezer Berkovits, "Jewish Living in America," *Judaism* 2 (January 1953): 70–71.
29. See Eliezer Berkovits, "A Contemporary Rabbinical School for Orthodox Jewry," *Tradition* 12 (Fall 1971): 6–7.
30. Eliezer Berkovits, "The Galut of Judaism," *Judaism* 4 (Summer 1955): 230. On Berkovits' concern over the secular-religious chasms in Israel, see Berkovits, "Like All the Nations?" *Jerusalem Post*, May 4, 1976, A29.

I am grateful to Rabbi Reuven Ziegler and Aryeh Grossman of Koren Publishers for inviting me to collect a volume of Eliezer Berkovits' writings. Koren's Ita Olesker supported this work through the very earliest stages and provided critical technical and editorial guidance. Together, Ita and I made sure that the text of each chapter conformed to Koren's style guide and issued slight editorial changes, while preserving the integrity of Eliezer Berkovits' writings and ideas. All modifications from the original works fall into three editorial categories: correction of obvious errors, insertion of paragraph breaks, and standardizing of transliteration and citations. This includes the use of the Koren Tanakh translation, sponsored by the Magerman family, that does much to improve the felicity of the text for modern readers. I am grateful to Yeshiva University for granting permission to reprint *Prayer* (1962), a pamphlet in its Studies in Torah Judaism series.

Thanks, as well, to Rabbi Dov Berkovits for inviting me to participate in a conference in September 2022 that commemorated his father's thirtieth yahrzeit. The opportunity to think afresh about Eliezer Berkovits' "anthropology" helped solidify this volume's contents and the themes of this introduction.

My understanding of Eliezer Berkovits' ideas and writings deepened while serving as professor and provost of Hebrew Theological College, a division of Touro University. In this way, and many others, Rabbi Berkovits' "home institution" remains a supporter of his legacy and teachings. Berkovits never taught at Gratz College in Melrose Park, Pennsylvania, where I now teach and serve as president. I hope this volume will catalyze a new effort to learn from and about Berkovits in the Greater Philadelphia area. Finally, as always, my wife, Melissa, and our three darling children – Meital, Jack, and Adir – stand as the guiding force in my life. I pray that our children will learn much from the pages that follow.

Zev Eleff

January 2023/Tevet 5783

Sources

"A Guest Feature." *Yeshiva Women* 7 (November 1958): 2–5.

"From the Temple to Synagogue and Back." *Judaism* 8 (Fall 1959): 303–11.

"God and National Existence," 66–75. In *Towards Historic Judaism*. Oxford: The East and West Library, 1943.

"God in History," 143–57. In *God, Man and History: A Jewish Interpretation*. New York: Jonathan David, 1959.

"Identity Problems in the State of Israel." *Judaism* 28 (Summer 1979): 334–44.

"In the Wilderness of the Nations," 116–21. In *Between Yesterday and Tomorrow*. Oxford: The East and West Library, 1945.

"Jewish Living in America." *Judaism* 2 (January 1953): 68–74.

"Philosophical and Theological Dimensions," *CCAR Year Book* 91 (1981): 104–10.

Prayer. New York: Yeshiva University, 1962.

"The Galut of Judaism." *Judaism* 4 (Summer 1955): 225–34.

"Toward Jewish Authenticity." *Jewish Spectator*, September 1953, 11–14.

Section 1

Prayer

From Temple to Synagogue and Back

One of the most far-reaching transformations in the history of Judaism was undoubtedly brought about by the destruction of the First Jewish Commonwealth and the Babylonian Exile that followed. It may be described as Judaism's way from the Temple to the synagogue. In accordance with Jewish teaching, the Temple was not to be rebuilt anywhere outside Jerusalem. Since the Temple service could not be practiced anywhere outside the Holy City, a new type of religious service had to take its place. The political conditions of the people effected the emergence of the synagogue. What was originally the makeshift arrangement of the *mikdash me'at,* the "Little Sanctuary," was turned into one of the most significant triumphs of Israel's religious genius. Thus, the great contribution of the Babylonian Exile to religious history was evolved. What were the salient features of the transformation which was accomplished by the creation of the synagogue?

The Temple service was a national institution, maintained by the State. The people paid for it, but they themselves were not actively associated with it. The daily sacrifices were offered by the priests on behalf of the people. The priests were the God-appointed representatives of the people. While the priests went about their duties in the Temple, the people pursued their daily tasks in the fields, in the workshops, in business and trade. God was worshipped professionally by a caste reserved and trained for the task. The average citizen was not expected to be familiar with the Temple ritual. In general, the people were the *am haaretz* and ignorant of the Torah. It was "the lips of the priests that kept knowledge."

It is of course proper to add that long before the destruction of Jerusalem there were developments afoot which pointed to new paths. There was, for instance, the institution of the *maamadot,* the daily assemblages of selected groups of men who met in prayer during the offering of the sacrifices in the Temple; nor were the priests the exclusive repositories of the knowledge of the Torah all the time. The decisive change, however, did not occur till the Babylonian Exile.

Of necessity, in Babylon prayer replaced the sacrifice. In its manifold consequences this development amounted to a major religious revolution. The sacrifice could only be offered by the priest; prayer was expected of everyone. Indeed, the delegation of one's duty to pray to a priest is unimaginable. Every Jew now became actively associated with the religious service. Looked at from the point of view of the people, in the Temple the divine service was mere ritual; in the synagogue it became a personalized religious endeavor. Religion turned inward toward the realm of individual commitment. Hand in hand with the growth in inwardness went the democratization of religious life. The priestly caste, the professionals of religion, lost their central significance. Every Jew was called upon to pray and to read the Torah in the synagogue.

No doubt, in the days of the Temple, too, the people took an intense interest in the service. Especially for the Holy Days they would come to Jerusalem from all parts of the country. But in the courtyards of the Temple they were *onlookers*; they were an audience, and the priests, the performers. In the synagogue, the audience was transformed into the praying community.

With deepening inwardness and religious democratization in the synagogue, Judaism became more and more the responsibility of the entire people. The "professionals" having been dispensed with, the knowledge of the Torah became a national obligation. The vicarious Temple service could rely on "the lips of the priests that keep knowledge";

the personalized responsibility of the religious democracy of the synagogue laid the emphasis on general education in the entire domain of Judaism. Thus, the *Beit HaKnesset* led to the *Beit HaMidrash*; the house of meeting became inseparable from the house of study.

It was unavoidable that a new type of a religious leader should arise. As the synagogue differed from the Temple so did the rabbi from the priest. The rabbi did not belong to a caste or a class; he was not a professional. In contrast to the priest, there were no religious duties for the rabbi which were not equally binding on all Jews. If the rabbi distinguished himself through his piety, he achieved something that was expected from every one of his fellow Jews. His learning and knowledge of the Torah might have rendered him outstanding, but only because he realized an ambition which he shared with all the people. The rabbi did not prepare himself for the rabbinate; like any other Jew, he prepared himself for the task of living in accordance with the Torah. For many centuries he was not salaried but earned his living like any other Jew, through farming, as an artisan or in trade and commerce. He most certainly was not a clergyman but the most representative layman of his community. He was the teacher who guided his fellow Jews along the path which they all had to follow together.

Such were the changes that shaped the historic image of Judaism since the days of the first Exile. For many centuries, and for the longest period of its history, Judaism has been Synagogue Judaism.

In modern times, and especially in this country, a turning away from the synagogue to a religious institution that is known as the temple has become a mark of progress. As I have indicated, compared with the Temple of old, the rise of the synagogue undoubtedly meant a radical transformation in the forward movement of Judaism. Does the modern temple lead beyond the synagogue or is it closer to the Temple of old? Does it bring the inherent motives of Judaism to more significant realization than the synagogue or does it show greater affinity to the spirit that prevailed in the Temple service of the distant past? Only the answer to this question can decide whether the temple of our days represents religious progress and is not a throwback to a more primitive form of religious practice.

If language and style are indicative of the spirit that is within a man, as indeed they are, one ought to say that the terminology, the vocabulary, that the modern temple has adopted makes it suspect of regression from the people's religion of the synagogue to the clericalism of the Temple of old. We no longer speak of the *shul* but of the sanctuary; it is no longer the *Beit HaMidrash* but the chapel (Webster says s.v. *chapel:* "... LL. *capella* orig., a short coat [cappa]; later, a reliquary, chapel [because the building where St. Martin's cloak was preserved came to be called "capella"]). There is no room in the temple for the modest *shulḥan of* the synagogue; we have the much more dignified altar instead. Everything in the temple seems to have added semantic weight. One does not pray in the temple, one worships; a temple Jew does not look for a *Minyan* to say Kaddish, he visits a chapel to recite a memorial prayer. No one ever sings in the temple but chants. The examples are manifold. The style of the modern temple seems to be reserved for the specific domain of piety. Everything seems to be consecrated and dedicated and set apart from everyday human interest and concern.

This is no mere affectation but reveals the essential quality of a certain type of religiosity. Modern Temple Judaism is indeed a thing apart from everyday human existence. As in days of yore, Temple Judaism is almost completely limited to the immediate precincts of the temple. It is an island of piety set in an ocean of secularism and materialism. The piety of the temple is unsupported by a living religious reality outside it. The holiness of the sanctuary does not go beyond the symbolic presentation of the idea in bricks and mortar. The altar is the elevating symbol of a sacrifice which is required of no one and which no one is prepared to offer. In these circumstances, style has to be pitched to a high note of solemn dignity. Temple Judaism cannot do without an inspirational vocabulary and consecrated props. Unrelated as it is to a living reality, all its religious emotions and thoughts have to be artificially induced by symbolic architecture and effect-producing interior decoration, by suggestive terminology and synthetic decorum. Everything is stimulated from without, nothing seeks expression from within. Everything is premeditated solemnity and mediated devotion.

On the other hand, the style of the synagogue is matter of fact; its accoutrements are essentially functional and not symbolical. This is due to the fact that the synagogue is an outgrowth of Jewish living. The divine service of the synagogue Jew takes place more outside the synagogue than inside it. The *Beit HaKnesset* is indeed a house of meeting, not really different in kind from other buildings; for wherever a Jew may find himself, he knows he is in the presence of God. In the *shul* too he is only continuing his life as a Jew. To pray to God together with the community is a task not essentially different from other tasks; for everything a man does is done in God's presence. A synagogue is not a sanctuary but the convenient place for the community to assemble for prayer. Whatever sanctity there is in the synagogue is in the living community and it originates chiefly in the life Jews lead outside the synagogue. Since the Torah is read in public, it is useful to have a *shulḥan,* a desk on which to place it. As to the altar, it has no place in the synagogue. Sacrifice is not a symbolical concept as it was in the Temple of old and as it is in the temple of our days, but is part of the daily discipline and practice of Jewish living. As Philo already said, the altar of God is the soul of man.

Compared with the Eternal Light of the Temple, even the *ner tamid of* the synagogue is only a functional object. As the phrase indicates, the Eternal Light is charged with the symbolism of eternity, which is thought to be most adequately expressed by expensive artistic design. The *ner tamid* of the synagogue, on the other hand, is a modest little lamp that serves as a reminder of the light which was kept burning nightly in the sanctuary in Jerusalem. Since it has no function beyond recalling memories of the past, the *ner tamid* is hardly ever noticed. It is certainly no symbol of eternity. It is not through "meaningful" lighting fixtures that Synagogue Judaism seeks contact with eternity.

Even such an exclusively "religious object" as the *aron hakodesh* is essentially functional in the synagogue. In the temple we speak of the Holy Ark, which is usually dramatized by the richest forms of deepest symbolical significance. Little edification indeed may be derived from the actual "reading of the law"; but exquisite design and meaningful artistry of the Holy Ark are extremely helpful in creating a devotional atmosphere. The *aron hakodesh,* however, should not be confused with the Holy Ark. The concern of the praying community is with the living word of the Torah. What need, and indeed what use, for Holy Ark symbolism beside the breath of the living spirit of the Torah! The *aron* is not an archaic Ark, which is useless from a practical point of view. The *aron* is a chest or a box, in which people keep all kinds of useful objects, books, clothes, jewels, and so forth. It has been set aside in the synagogue to place the Torah in it for safekeeping till the next occasion of reading and study. As the grammatical form proves, *aron hakodesh* is not the holy chest but the chest of the holy. In the synagogue, an empty *aron* is useless; in the temple, the inspirational effect of the Holy Ark symbolism would remain potent even if the "Scrolls of the Law" were exchanged for a copy of the by-laws of the temple congregation.

Undoubtedly, Synagogue Judaism does associate the idea of holiness with objects and buildings. However, as the phrase by which these objects are known itself indicates, the *tashmishei kedusha* receive a degree of holiness from the use to which they are put. As the tools of a purpose that aims at the sanctification of all life, they become consecrated through usage and not through glittering dedicatory exercises. The longer they serve the more venerable they become. The creation of an atmosphere of devotion by means of clever architectonic ideas is unnatural in the synagogue. But if such an atmosphere, a *genius loci* as it were, should exist, as well it may and often does, it could only be as the lingering on of the accumulated memories of the religious life of preceding generations. The sanctuary, the chapel, the altar, and so forth, of the modern temple are appointed to convey a message of sanctity to hesitant hearts. They are at the height of their effectiveness when they are still new; wear and tear undermines the dignity of these kinds of symbols.

The *Alte Shul* was the pride of a Jewish community, which would surround it with love as if the old building were a living being. In our days, an old temple is shunned as casting a reflection on the social status of those associated with it, as if they could not afford something newer and better.

In this connection it may be appropriate to make some observations on the subject of religious art as well as religious symbolism.

Notwithstanding the efforts that are being made to bring beauty to temple buildings and their interior appointments as well as to bestow artistic value on the religious objects used in the temple, the results are often disappointing and at best of questionable quality. And how could it be otherwise? Beauty is truth because, as Plato saw it long before Keats, it mirrors in the world of material objects a vision of the soul. It is always an ideal, a truth, alive first in his soul, that the artist attempts to impart to his material. Religious art stems from a religious vision, from a religious faith that is intense enough to long for expression. In Judaism the expression of the vision was sought preeminently in living. The aesthetic needs of the Jew were better satisfied in the dynamism of beautiful deeds than in the static harmony of beautiful forms. Nevertheless, it was unavoidable that the spirit that used the *tashmishei kedusha* should become reflected in them in aesthetic form, as well.

Wherever the vision of the soul touches the world of things, beauty is born. The art of the synagogue, which had a long and significant history in the old Jewries of Europe, made visible the reality of religious inwardness in the life of the Jew. But whence is genuine religious art to come in the modern temple? Where is the religious vision, where the overflowing religious faith straining for artistic expression, where the religious reality from which new artistic concepts may emanate? Of course, for money one may always buy the services of outstanding architects and reputable artists. But unlike the cathedral builders of the Middle Ages, these modern temple builders are not as deeply inspired by faith that the religious truth which dwells in their souls could stimulate them to creativity in the field of religious art. Occasionally, they may incorporate in their designs some abstract idea of a personal metaphysics, which may even be admired by the initiated members of the congregation as one admires a museum exhibit. At best, the architects and the artists will copy; they will imitate old synagogue motifs or new church designs. Alas, only all too often the final impression is that of expensive glitter and tinsel. When a modern temple grows old it becomes indeed a shabby thing.

Not altogether dissimilar is the value of temple symbolism. Great religions often cannot do without symbols. When the spirit of man beholds a supreme reality which it cannot name articulately, symbols may be justified. Even though their status in Judaism is questionable, man's need for them may be readily acknowledged. When the religious person has exhausted all his resources trying to express the truth he knows, he may use symbols to hint at the transcendental being which he cannot or dare not address in a manner commensurate with its essence. The symbols of the temple, however, stand in a religious vacuum no less than its art. They do not point from the highest rung of religious awareness at that which lies beyond our reach but hint timidly at what ought to be expressed in human life and which the modern Jew does not care to bring to realization. The sanctuary, the chapel, the altar, the eternal light, the Holy Ark, the entire "consecrated style," are substitutes for religious living. As temple art is mainly tinsel, so are temple symbols essentially make-believe.

The symbols of the temple are calculated to evoke devotional reaction from the worshipper; the tools of sanctification in the synagogue, however, reflect the living purpose of the spirit that uses them. Symbolism proposes to elicit religious meditation from without; sanctification proceeds from within man to the external world of objects and places. The one is as distinct from the other as is religious ritual from religious living. It is of the very essence of the ritual that it employs places, objects, and gestures attempting to make an impact on the realm of the spirit. Religious living, on the other hand, begins in the innermost recesses of the spirit of man and strives to impart its purpose to the realm of outside reality. Temple Judaism, unsupported as it is by religious living outside the temple, is ritualistic. In essence it is nearer to the cults, charms, and incantations of primitive religions than to the revolutionary transformation that the synagogue accomplished when it made Judaism the possession of all Israel.

The ritualistic nature of Temple Judaism finds its clear manifestation in the most significant feature of temple architecture. The basic architectural difference between temple and synagogue is that whereas the synagogue has a center, the temple has none. In the center of the synagogue stands the *shulḥan* or *bima,* the place for the *shaliaḥ tzibbur* as well as for the reading of the Torah in public. It is natural for the praying community to organize itself around a central point. It is in the midst of the people that the word of God comes to life and it is from its midst that the prayer of all ascends. The *shaliaḥ tzibbur* is not "leading us in prayer"; he is the unifying focus through which the numerous individual prayers are woven into the prayer of the community. The synagogue is essentially a *round house.* The Temple in Jerusalem was a long structure. The courtyard faced the sanctuary, the sanctuary looked toward the Holy of Holies. The more important points of interest were in front of the less important ones. This was a natural arrangement, as it is always where the few perform for the many, as in the theater, the lecture hall, the political meeting place. The stage, the dais, the platform are logically in front of the spectators. In all these cases the "long house" is the structural sign of the inner purpose.

So it was in the Temple of old, where the priests performed their duties on behalf of the people; and so it seems to be in the temple of our own days. The place of worship has reverted from the "round house" to the "long house." The important points of interest have been moved to the elevated platform in front of the congregants. It is there that, like some mystery cult, the essential parts of the service are enacted by the initiated functionaries of the temple. The congregants are in the main audience; as in the Temples of old, they have once again become onlookers. It is true that the professionals of the cult make desperate efforts to encourage the onlookers to become participants. However, participation remains forever vague, colorless, and superficial. It dies away completely as soon as the goading and coaxing directives from the "platform" come to an end. The religious democracy of the praying community of the synagogue, with its immediacy and great moments of spontaneity, is lost. The ugly interruptions of the temple service by the continuous announcing of the pages in the prayer book, decorously performed by the religious experts on the platform, has become part of an ideology. It is indicative of the secrets of a ritual with which only the initiated few may be familiar.

There is no way from the temple to the *Beit HaMidrash.* As in times of Jewish antiquity, once again the religious officials have become the repositories of all knowledge about Judaism. The religious experts of the modern temple are known as rabbis, which however is a misnomer. Judged by their functions and specific status, they are much closer to the priests of bygone days than to the rabbis of the synagogue. They are the professional keepers of the mysteries; they are like intermediaries, long since abolished in the synagogue, between the people and their God. It was unavoidable that the modern temple should have revived the archaic custom of clothing its functionaries in priestly vestment. In the synagogue the rabbi wears the *tallit* like anyone else in the congregation; in the temple the religious functionary is marked out by the clerical garb. Unlike the rabbi, he is not one of the community, but one set apart from the rest of the people.

One hears a great deal these days about Judaism being a way of life. The truth of course is that for the overwhelming majority of modern Jews, Judaism is not a way at all but ceremony reserved for specific occasions. It is not the case that the modern Jew – as he likes to flatter himself – is anti-ritualistic. On the contrary, he is ritual-struck. With a sense of self-righteous superiority, he cuts himself loose from the traditions of his people and from the faith of his fathers; but with what childish self-forgetfulness does he not delve into the mysteries of the secret ritual of his lodge! The same Jew who unperturbed by his abysmal ignorance of all things Jewish, easily dismisses religious practices as mere ceremony, will with a deep sense of gratification deck himself out with masonic insignia and perform the prescribed ceremonial with a solemnity and earnestness worthy of a Corybant. Our temples, too, are the veritable breeding grounds of new-fangled ceremonies and rituals. Never before have Jews indulged so intensely in candle lighting as they do today. A candle-lighting ceremony never lets you down. Numberless are the variations of the initiation-of-new-members ceremony as well as of the installation-of-new-officers ritual. No self-respecting temple will be without the dedication-of-the-first-year-students-of-the-Hebrew-School celebration.

The consecration service ritual is usually prepared, rehearsed, and enacted by the modern Jew with hardly less devotion than that with which his ancestors were wont to observe the Sabbath or, perhaps, even Yom Kippur. Except that with the modern Jew it all starts and ends in the temple. It is all solemn and symbolic but unrelated to real life and therefore superficial – a mere phantom.

Is, however, our analysis not belied by the religious revival which seems to be sweeping American Jewry? Unfortunately, all the characteristic marks of faith and piety are lacking in this revival. In all our magnificent temples one would look in vain for the "broken spirit" and the "contrite heart," without which one may hardly find one's way to God. There is no convincing sign of the modern Jew's willingness to submit to God, of his preparedness to accept the *ol Malkhut Shamayim,* the yoke of the Kingdom of God, which is to be established on this earth. The religious concepts of *yirat Shamayim* and *ahavat Hashem,* of the fear and the love of God, are foreign to him. One discerns very little respect indeed for the authority of the spirit and the relevance of its standards for the life of man. The modern Jew's revived interest in Judaism is sociological and psychological; it has little to do with religion proper.

Strangely enough, the reawakened interest in Judaism is often a sign of assimilation. Within the climate of American culture, religion has become a sign of respectability. For some mythical reason an atheist is not considered a trustworthy citizen. And so Jews, caught by the fever of conformity, remembered that they too had a religion. Since, however, to have a religion is essentially a matter of social convention, it is sufficient to have it symbolically, without going to all the trouble of making it a way of life in earnest. One respects conventions in order to show that one belongs to the class of "the right people," but to overdo it would be in bad taste. It is an observation worth pondering that whereas in the ghettos of former days one could occasionally meet a convinced *apikoros,* in American Jewry one hardly ever comes across a genuine atheist. We are all believers, because religion is no longer for us a matter of vital conviction but a mere mark of social status. We are as religious as we are inclined to conform to the standards of our middle-class mass culture. We shall be justified in looking for religious revival when American Jewry will produce its own articulate atheists. It will be a sign that religion has ceased being a matter of indifference and has gained sufficient interest to be worthwhile rejecting. Our present affirmations are of little religious significance. We do not confess God but give a nod to the social convention that it is proper to confess a God, some God, any God.

Psychologically our religious revival is to be a cure-all for our anxieties. Religion has become a substitute for the couch of the psychoanalyst. It is expected to give us peace of mind, to bring us happiness, to guarantee us good health, and to assure us of never-ending prosperity. This religion is not God-oriented but man-centered; man is not required to serve God, but God is meant to serve man. It is the typical religion of a comfortable middle class. We have everything now: jobs, professions, homes, cars, insurance policies; and we also *have* a God.

It is useful to have a God; one can never tell when one may need Him. Our religion is a prop for our prosperity and comforts. No one is concerned with the word of God; no one listens and no one obeys. The function of our awakened piety is to confirm us in our habits and our customary way of thought. We believe in God, but we also limit His authority. We prescribe for Him how to act toward us. Truth for Him is what *we* hold to be true; right what *we* consider right. He can ask of us no more than what we ask of ourselves. Most important of all, He is to be considerate; in no way may He inconvenience us or interfere with our comforts and pleasures. The essential quality of this religiosity is that man does not practice what he believes but believes what he practices. We believe in God after having shaped Him in our image. It is a religion cut to measure to suit us. It is not a way of life but a means to affirm to ourselves our own way of living. And since our way of living is basically secular, it is the misuse of the sign of the spirit in order to lend security and dignity to the materialism of our concept of life. It is religion without any significant spiritual content. It represents a rejection of the authority of the spirit and an attempt to transform it into a magic force to be harnessed to the drives of our self-seeking.

The quality of our religious revival illustrates the motivating impulse behind the regression from synagogue to temple. Because the main function of religion has become a confirmation for us of our way of living, and since no interference with our life practices may be tolerated, Judaism has been relegated back to the precincts of the temple and limited to specific observances of specific occasions. Because the authority of the spirit is rejected, one may admit only symbols of the spiritual. Since the modern Jew is concerned only with the effects of the symbols, all that is left is ritual and ceremony. Before there may be any new religious growth in our midst, we shall have to find our way back to the position which was attained by us when we moved on from the Temple to the synagogue. We have a long way to go.

What Is Jewish Prayer?

Prayer would seem to be as natural to religion as breathing is to all living things. The overflowing of the heart, which finds its expression in hymns and praises, in intercession or thanksgiving, is of the very essence of the life of religion. Religion without prayer is like music without melody, like dark clouds over the sun-parched earth yielding no rain. Yet, prayer is also religion's most problematic child. The problems are numerous. They may be of a philosophical nature. Kant, for instance, considered it "an absurd and presumptuous delusion" that "by the insistent importunity of prayer" men might deflect God from "the plan of His wisdom" in order "to provide some momentary advantage for us."[1]

From the philosophical point of view, it is equally difficult to fathom how man, a finite being, may confront the Infinite or Absolute, as is purported to be the case in prayer. However, objections to certain types of prayers are raised not only on philosophical or theological grounds, but also with the very fervor of religious faith. At times, the very intensity of one's religious belief will not let one pray. The German mystic Eckhart created the parable of the sick man who would not pray to God to make him well for three reasons. He was sure that God would

1. See Friedrich Heiler, *Prayer: A Study in the History and Psychology of Religion*, trans. Samuel McComb (London: Oxford University Press, 1932), 89.

never allow him to fall sick unless it were for his own good. He would, therefore, not pray for the removal of what was in his own interest. He also reasoned that since he was sick, it must have been the will of God that it be so. To pray for health would be praying against God's will. It is not for man to ask God to adjust His will to man's desire, but rather to adjust the human wish to the divine will. Finally, he argued, God being infinitely powerful and perfect, the health of a little creature like a human being may indeed be a small matter in His sight. He concluded, therefore, that he "ought not to pray the rich and loving God for such trifles."[2] On the strength of such faith-inspired reasoning religious mystics in all ages and many religions would refuse to pray for this-worldly goods and would ask God for only the most noble gifts, like the revelation of His presence, communion with Him, or – as a Persian mystic put it – they beg "from God as a gift God Himself."[3]

Undisturbed by the metaphysical, theological, and religious problems of prayer, Jews through the ages have prayed for the trifling needs of human existence as well as the noblest aspirations of the soul and of the spirit that is within man. Undisturbed by the problems, we say; but not unaware of them. Jews knew well that *nireh raḥok*, that to all philosophical and metaphysical appearances, the Absolute was far removed from involvement with the finite sphere of man, yet they prayed; because they also knew that the Absolute was God, *veHu karov* and as such He was near, indeed the nearest to man (*Midrash Tehillim* 4:1). They were forever conscious of their own nothingness in the presence of the Infinite. For "what were they, what their life, or their good deeds, what their strength and might" in the sight of the One before whom "even the mightiest among men are like naught and even the men of renown as if they had never been or the wise as if without knowledge." How, indeed, could they address themselves to Him? Yet, they approached and came near and addressed the All-Wise with the foolish words of their own creaturely insignificance without letup, scandalously calling the Lord "our God and God of our fathers." Not for a moment were they forgetful of the universal laws of heaven and earth which were established in God's

2. Ibid., 192.
3. Ibid.

infinite wisdom, of the cosmic plan and purpose which are inherent in all creation, yet they forever importuned Him with their prayers in order to make Him change His plan or will. They stood in awe before a divine decree, yet in their prayers, they never ceased to attempt "to tear it up." All through the ages, the martyrs of Israel in their myriads sanctified the name of God by accepting His unfathomable will and surrendering of their lives to Him, asking for nothing, only confessing: "Hear, O Israel, the Lord, our God, the Lord is the Only One"; yet, they never ceased declaring also in the words of the psalmist: "He fulfills the desire of them that fear Him," or in the words of the Talmud: "The righteous decrees and God fulfills." Their whole life, as Jews, was dedicated to the task of obeying God's law and doing His bidding, yet, in their prayers, they often – rather unseemingly – demanded that their will be done by God.

To our mind, the reconciliation of such opposing tendencies and conflicting ideas is the unique achievement of Jewish prayer. It superbly meets the problems of praying without sacrificing the naive simplicity of the trusting, God-ward turned human being.

What is Jewish prayer?

How Is Prayer Possible?

At times, prayer is described as an unburdening of the soul, a pouring out of the heart. This in itself might be psychologically significant and useful. It represents, however, only one aspect of prayer. Hannah, the childless wife of Elkanah, who unintentionally became one of the classic teachers of right praying in Judaism, said of herself, "I poured out my soul before the Lord." In a number of other places in the Bible, prayer is referred to in a similar way. After the fall of Jerusalem, the prophet, Jeremiah, demands of Israel, "pour out your heart like water before God." The psalmist calls to prayer in the words "Pour out your heart before Him." Prayer is the pouring out of the heart before God; it is not a soliloquy. In prayer, one stands before God. Only when one addresses oneself to God does one pray. But how does one know that one is not soliloquizing? How does one know that one stands, indeed, before God?

Something paradoxical seems to be implied in the situation of confronting God in prayer. Pouring out one's heart before God, does one have an actual experience of the presence of God, does one actually behold God as one's vis-à-vis? It would seem to us that when this occurs, prayer has reached its penultimate goal. In the rare moments when the rarest among great religious personalities experience and confront the Divine Presence, all human needs disappear and all prayer has been fulfilled. After the experience, recalling it in memory, one may break forth in jubilation and thanksgiving; during the experience, however, wishless silence would seem to be the natural attitude. In prayer man searches for the Divine Presence, yet one may search for it only by turning to the Divine Presence. The more intense the experience of being forsaken by God, the more fervent the prayer for God's nearness; yet, one can pray to Him because He is near. Only to a God who is near may one call, "Why, Lord, do You stand far off, hiding Yourself in times of trouble?" (Ps. 10:1). Only in His presence can one complain to Him about His absence, only to His face may one weep in prayer for His hiding of the face.

How then is prayer possible? If the distance from the Divine Presence is the stimulus of prayer, if the estrangement between God and man is the source of its need, if the hiding of the face by God is responsible for the outpouring of the heart, how can one pray, since man must stand in God's presence when he prays?

The manner in which the basic requirement for man's attitude in prayer has been formulated in the Talmud (Sanhedrin 22a) may well be the pointer to the resolution of the dilemma. It is said: "He who prays should consider himself as if the Divine Presence were confronting him, for so did the psalmist exclaim: 'I have set the Lord always before me.'" The statement seems to weaken our premise that in prayer man stands before God. Rabbi Shimon Ḥasida, the author of the saying, speaks of the confrontation as if it occurred; man should look upon himself as if he were faced by the DivinePresence.

In my opinion, the use of the phrase "as if" gives a succinct expression to the paradoxical nature of the praying attitude. Prayer takes its origin from a loss of intimacy with God, from the actual experience of God's hidden face. How then can man, in the midst of his experience that God is hiding Himself from him, that He is not present for him, that his "ways are hidden from the Lord," how can he step forward into the Divine Presence and ask for relief from the crushing experience of the non-Divine Presence? There is only one way of doing it: notwithstanding the negative personal experience, to turn to God as if He were present and to pour out one's heart before Him for His "absence." This can be done, maintains Rabbi Shimon the Ḥasid, and the result is not a situation of make-believe. The support which he finds in the words of the psalmist explains his meaning.

When King David said, "I have set the Lord always before me," he was of course not speaking of the specific occasions of prayer. The word "always" indicates that he was referring to something that was going on continually. He had in mind his entire life, all the activities of his everyday existence. All the time, he set the Lord before him. The psalmist gave expression here to the very essence of Jewish religiosity. Judaism implies the affirmation that God is forever present, that all life is enacted in His sight. Therefore, it is man's responsibility to set this truth always before him; to live all the days of his life and to perform every one of his deeds with the awareness that it all takes place in the presence of God. Only because of that is prayer possible in Judaism. Without it, the confrontation in prayer would indeed be a mere as-if situation.

From the individual experience of God's remoteness alone, one cannot step forward into the Divine Presence and ask for the elimination of the distance. God is not present *when* man prays to Him; man may pray to Him because He is the always-present God. Out of the midst of the personal experience of God's hidden face, one faces God *as if* His face were not hidden from one. It is, indeed, an as-if situation in relationship to one's personal experience; but it is not a situation of make-believe, for God is indeed always present and near. The confrontation may not always be subjectively real, yet it is objectively true. Only because it is objectively valid may, in the fulfillment of prayer, the as-if confrontation ripen more and more into a personal experience of the Divine Presence.

One may confront God in prayer because all life is a confrontation between God and man. Living with the awareness of the Divine Presence, man is God-ward turned. Every undertaking of such a man has something of the nature of an offering to God; it is a prayer enacted. Thus, when praying, the Jew is asked to consider himself confronting the Divine Presence. He is not required to enter into a specific situation of prayer, but by the specific means of prayer to become acutely aware of the human situation of living in the presence of God. Prayer, in Judaism, is not an activity apart from life, but a specific form of the Jewish way of life. In Judaism, living means facing God. One lives in the attitude of prayer and one prays in the attitude of living.

In which sense do I call prayer a specific form of Jewish living? Is it a more intense form of confrontation, does it establish a more intimate relationship between man and God? Within the framework of Judaism, it is difficult to agree to the suggestion. One may *pray* with little awareness of the Divine Presence, just as some unusual religious personalities have *lived* in ever-renewed intimacy with it. Theoretically, it is possible for one to be a pious Jew in the strictest Orthodox sense of the word without ever uttering a word of prayer. Those of whom it may be said that *Toratan umanutan,* that the study of the Torah is their sole life occupation, do not have to pray. This is not so because one can live as a Jew without prayer, but because whatever one does fulfilling oneself as a Jew is not essentially different from praying. For many generations, numberless Jews studying the pages of the Talmud have experienced the nearness of God, and have had a sense of intimacy with Him, not surpassed in intensity by the prayer of the most devout. Sitting at the Sabbath meal, as a part of the sanctification of the day of rest, Jews may have a realization of living under the providential eyes of God no less intense than any which might be accomplished by the means of prayer. A Jew preoccupied with the performance of a mitzva does not need to interrupt his activity for the sake of prayer. Any deed performed in the name of God is not essentially different from prayer. In the mitzva one may confront God no less than in prayer.

While the attitude of standing in the Divine Presence is the same in Jewish praying as in Jewish living, one might perhaps describe the difference between the two in the following manner. Living as a Jew, one meets the world in the name of God; one turns to God by acting on the world with the awareness of God. In prayer, one does not meet the world, one withdraws from the outside. In Jewish living, we turn God-ward with what we do to the world; in praying, we face God with what the world has done to us. In living, we seek His Divine Presence with what we are giving to life; in praying, with what we have received from it. Living as a Jew, one draws near by one's action; praying, by one's endurance.

We shall appreciate the fuller significance of this if we take another glance at the as-if situation which I have discussed earlier. Both praying and living have in common the need of being undertaken as if one were confronting the Divine Presence. I have mentioned the paradoxical element in prayer; so is there one in living, too. All life takes place in the presence of God, all life is confrontation with God. This is a truth without which Judaism is not possible. However, most of the time, in actual personal experience of living one faces the world and not God. Here, too, there is a discrepancy between the subjective life experience and the objective truth. God is present, but His presence is most of the time not experienced. The ever-present God is a silent God. Thus, a Jew has to meet the world as if, facing it and acting on it, he were facing and acting toward God. One can do it because, no matter what one's personal subjective experience of the world may be, in actual fact one stands under the inquisitively watching eyes of God.

Living as a Jew implies a twofold confrontation; one faces the world, and one faces God. Facing the world is the subjectively valid experience of living; facing God is the objectively valid affirmation of Judaism. As a Jew practices facing the world as if he were facing God in subjectively convincing experience, as a result of his Jewish living he will be led into the Divine Presence. But praying too implies a twofold confrontation. As man seeks God with what the world has done to him, he does not face the world; he faces himself. Attempting to approach God with what he has endured, he must have begun with an act of self-confrontation. In living, the original experience is meeting the world; the original experience that leads to praying is meeting oneself. In the act of living, one is preoccupied with the confrontation with the world; in the situation of enduring prior to prayer, one is in loneliness preoccupied with oneself. As in living, preoccupation with the world may blot out the awareness of the Divine Presence, so preoccupation with oneself may forever close the gates of prayer against oneself. Therefore, the task is always the same – to set the Lord always before oneself: in Jewish living, to transform the confrontation with the world into a confrontation with God; in Jewish praying, to move from the island of self-confrontation into the living Divine Presence of God.

Needless to say that in what has been said thus far a certain concept of God is implied. One cannot go out in search of the presence of Aristotle's First Cause. One cannot confront either the Infinite or the Absolute. One can live and pray only in the presence of the living personal God of Judaism. We know about Him not by philosophical derivation or by metaphysical insight or intuition. We know Him because He made Himself known to us. We know Him from historic experience, from His numerous manifestations in the history of Israel, from the revelation at Sinai, from His intercourse with the prophets, from His occasional manifestations within the life of unique personalities who in all generations live in His presence. Man may confront God because God has first confronted man and called His creature into confrontation with Him.

The infinite is indeed unapproachable, but the Infinite approached man in the history of Judaism and invited man to approach Him. Man, on his own, could never have done it; he can do it only because God has made it known to him that He is an accessible God. The Absolute cannot be faced by mere man; only God could make it possible for man to face Him. Judaism is God's invitation to man to live in the presence of the Almighty. Man may live in His presence because God desires him so to live. Man may seek God's closeness in prayer because God has made Himself known as the One who is close. Man may call on Him, because He desires to be called by man. "God is desirous of the prayers of Israel" (*Midrash Tehillim* 116:2); this is the foundation of the possibility of Jewish prayer. The Jew can pray because God has "opened his lips." Yehuda HaLevi said of Judaism that it was begun by God, meaning that it was not a human discovery but a religion of revelation; it commenced with God's self-revelation. So is prayer in Judaism not the original creation of man but made possible by God who lets us come near by being near us. There is a temptation to compare revelation and prayer and to say that in revelation God addresses man, whereas in prayer man addresses God. One must overcome the temptation; it all begins with revelation. It is true that in revelation, God seeks man, and in prayer, man seeks God. However, man may seek God only because he knows that He may be found; and he knows that God may be found because he was first found by God.

These considerations reveal to us another significant feature of Jewish prayer. Prayer is a most intimate experience that takes place between man and his Maker. It is intensely personal. In prayer, we open our heart before God as we would never do before a fellow man. Yet, within Judaism one can pray only in the context of the Jewish historic experience with the world and with God. The individual experience alone is not sufficient for prayer. Standing by oneself, in the loneliness of self-confrontation and in remoteness from the Divine Presence, how could the individual break through into the Divine Presence, asking for its manifestation? In the hour of need, when God has turned His face from the individual, how can he, left altogether to his own resources, pray – as he must – *as if* he confronted the Divine Presence and yet be sure that the confrontation is not a mere figment of his imagination? How can he be certain that the God who is hiding His face from him is not a non-present God, not an impersonal Absolute or Infinite; how can he know that he is not soliloquizing; indeed, how can he pray? How can he resolve the paradox of prayer, seeking the Divine Presence in the midst of the visitation of non-Divine Presence by turning to the Divine Presence? Of course, it is conceivable that the individual himself should have a direct personal experience of confrontation with God, but – as we saw earlier – those rarest of occasions are moments of breathless human silence. One calls to God "out of the depth."

In the light of a purely individualistic religion, one will either have a sufficiently overwhelming experience of the Divine Presence to sustain one all through life or the experience will not be sufficiently sustaining and will allow one to sink again and again back into the depth. In the first case, one will not pray but jubilantly contemplate the glory that confronts one. However, if the individual experience is too weak to support a lasting conviction of an ever-present God, whom will one be able to call "out of the depth"? On the basis of a completely personal religion, one either need not pray or can only soliloquize.[1] The overwhelming majority of human beings, of course, do not have the knowledge of the continuous confrontation as the result of actual personal experience.

1. A great deal of sophistication of the prayer of some mystics has its origin in this dilemma.

Even King David, the incomparable master of prayer, had occasion to exclaim: "For how long, Lord, will You forget me? Forever?" (Ps. 13:2); even he could not suppress the experience of non-Divine Presence, as he called in the bitterness of his heart, "O God, my God – why have You forsaken me? So far from my salvation are the words that I roar" (Ps. 22:2). The entire paradoxical situation of prayer comes to full expression in this passage. The psalmist's personal experience is that he is "forgotten forever," that he is forsaken by God and God is far removed from his cry, yet he addresses himself to God *as if* he were confronting the Divine Presence. He is forgotten "forever"; yet he knows it is only a question of how long, because, notwithstanding the personal experience, God does not forget anyone. God does not hear his cry, yet it is to this God who does not hear him that he turns with his plea, expecting to be heard about not being heard. He can do it because his personal experience is integrated with the entire historic experience of Israel. What is denied to individual experience is affirmed by the historic manifestations of the Divine Presence that called Israel into being and has sustained it through the ages. Because of it, a man completely abandoned by God may turn to God who does not abandon any one of His children. Prayer is needed because of the individual experience; it is possible because of the collective experience of all Israel. Because God is "our God and the God of our fathers," a Jew overwhelmed by the tragic personal knowledge of having been forsaken forever may yet address Him with the intimacy of "My God, my God."

Prayer and the Needs of Man

Prayer is not only a posture, an attitude of confrontation with God. In prayer people plead with God. Prayer has contents in which man asks God for the fulfillment of his needs. The objects of our requests in prayer have been subjected to critical scrutiny by philosophers and mystics alike. Philosophers have scoffed at prayer which has "eudaemonistic" goals, that asks for material or physical benefits and aims at personal happiness. One should pray only for the moral good and for the power to act and live virtuously. Mystics went even further. They often believed that even such "trifles" were not really worthy to be asked for of the great God. When standing before Him, one should ask only for the greatest boon, i.e., the enjoyment of God Himself, of His nearness, of the communion with Him. Judaism is not unfamiliar with these noble aims of philosophical or mystical prayer.

There is hardly another prayer on record which is so desperately concerned with one's spiritual shortcoming than the fifty-first psalm:

> To the lead singer – a psalm of David,
> when the prophet Natan came to him
> after he came to Batsheva.

Show me grace, God, in Your loyalty;
in Your great mercy, erase my offense;
wash me well of my guilt;
purify me of my sin,
for I am aware of my transgression,
and my sin is ever before me.
I sinned against You alone;
I committed what is evil in Your eyes,
so Your sentence is just,
and Your judgment is fair.
Yes, with guilt I came to be;
in sin did my mother conceive me.
Yes, You desire truth to course deep within me –
to teach wisdom to my innermost self.
Purge me with hyssop, and I will be pure;
wash me, and I will be whiter than snow.
Let me hear gladness and joy;
let the bones You have crushed rejoice.
Hide Your face from my sins;
erase all my guilt.
Create a pure heart for me, God;
renew a firm spirit within me.

Nor is the mystic longing for the Divine Presence unknown to Jewish prayer. Has it been expressed more movingly than, for instance, in the words of the forty-second psalm?

As a deer pines for flowing streams,
my soul pines for You, God;
my soul thirsts for God, the living God –
oh, when will I come and appear before God?...
Why are you miserable, my soul?
Why do you grieve so within me?
Hope for God –
that I will yet praise Him
in the salvation of His presence.

Or consider some verses of the seventy-third psalm:

> Yet I am always with You;
> You hold my right hand.
> You guide me with Your counsel;
> You take me toward glory.
> Whom else do I have in heaven?
> With You, I desire nothing else on earth.
> Though my flesh and heart waste away,
> God is the Rock of my heart
> and my portion forever...
> but as for me,
> God's closeness is good for me.
> I have made the Lord God my refuge,
> to tell of all Your works.

Though these are the outpourings of an individual heart, they voice the search and the longing of the Jewish soul. Only in the context of the religious life of all Israel could one pray as the psalmist did. Jewish prayer is impregnated with the sentiments and aspirations of the psalms, just as so many of them have been incorporated in the Prayer Book of the Jewish people. Nevertheless, notwithstanding this remarkable appreciation of the noblest of goods, the Jew has never been reticent to pray also for those lesser blessings which were treated somewhat contemptuously by philosophers and mystics. In the *Shemoneh Esreh* we commence our series of requests with prayer for understanding, for return to God, and for forgiveness of sins; but we continue, without the slightest hesitation, and pray for redemption from personal afflictions, for healing from sickness, for an adequate livelihood. Three times a day, we pray for the establishment of the world as a Kingdom of God, yet we also ask for the ingathering of the exiles of our people and the restoration of Zion. Some of the noblest universalistic prayers of mankind are enunciated by Israel during the holiest days of the Jewish year. On those days we pray:

> And so place the fear of You, Lord our God,
> over all that You have made,

> and the terror of You over all You have created,
> and all who were made will stand in awe of You,
> and all of creation will worship You,
> and they will be bound all together as one
> to carry out Your will with an undivided heart;
> for we know, Lord our God,
> that all dominion is laid out before You,
> strength is in Your palm, and might in Your right hand,
> Your name spreading awe over all You have created.
> Our God and God of our ancestors,
> rule over all the world in Your honor,
> and be raised above all the earth in Your glory,
> and appear, in the splendor of Your great might
> before all those who live in this world, Your domain.
> And all who were made will know that You made them,
> and all who were formed will know that You formed them,
> and all that have breath in their mouths will declare:
> The Lord, God of Israel, is King,
> and His kingship has dominion over all.

Nevertheless, practically in the same breath, we also pray:

> And so place honor, Lord, upon Your people,
> praise on those who fear You and hope into those who seek You,
> the confidence to speak into all who long for You,
> gladness to Your land and joy to Your city,
> the flourishing of pride to David Your servant,
> and a lamp laid out for his descendant, Your anointed,
> soon, in our days.

Jewish prayer covers every area of human life, the material as well as the spiritual, the personal as well as the social, the national as well as the universal. Jewish prayer shows no less appreciation of moral and spiritual values than some of the most significant tomes of the philosophers, yet a Jew prays unabashedly for his daily bread as well as for the needs of the spirit. A deep and fervent longing for the manifestation of the Divine

Presence comes to expression in the prayer of the Jew, yet he will quite naturally also pray for salvation from the hands of his enemies, and see nothing incongruous in such praying. How are such apparent contradictory tendencies to be reconciled with each other? Anticipating the result of our discussion on this point, and putting it – as it were – in a nutshell, we should say that they are to be reconciled through – prayer.

The philosopher who would pray to God only for moral and spiritual goods misunderstands completely the situation in which man confronts God in prayer. Of course, there are differences between the various values of men; there are higher and lower goods, and man should always aspire to the nobler things in life. But prayer is not a dissertation on ethics; nor is it possible for a man to pray standing on ethical principles alone. As we turn to God in prayer, do we mean to make an impression on Him with the nobility of our aspirations? Do we mean to prevail upon Him by asking for the power to do good rather than for the strength to breathe and walk and work? Nothing could be more naive and less philosophical. There is indeed an order of values down here, which has meaning in relationship to man. But what is the significance of this order of human values in relationship to God? When the mystic refuses to pray for mere trifles, he should stop praying altogether. For even the noblest of man's desires, the mystical communion with God, is only a human desire and, perhaps, a mere trifle in the sight of God. Can one really maintain that a philosopher or a mystic has a greater claim to God's attention than the lowliest of His creatures? As far as our dignity is concerned in the presence of God, it is correctly summed up in a passage of Judaism's daily prayers:

> Master of all worlds,
> not because of our righteousness
> do we lay our pleas before You,
> but because of Your great compassion.
> What are we? What are our lives?
> What is our loving-kindness? What is our righteousness?
> What is our salvation? What is our strength?
> What is our might? What shall we say before You,
> Lord our God and God of our ancestors?

> Are not all the mighty like nothing before You,
> the men of renown as if they had never been,
> the wise as if they know nothing,
> and the understanding as if they lack intelligence?
> For their many works are in vain,
> and the days of their lives like a fleeting breath before You.
> The preeminence of man over the animals is nothing,
> for all is but a fleeting breath.

That mere man should be able to confront God is logically inconceivable. Yet, it is a fact; however – as we have seen in the previous chapter – not because man can approach God, but because, in His unfathomable mercy, God has approached man. Was He induced to do so by the nobility of human aspirations? What impact may all the goodness of man make on the Infinite? It is with our need alone that we may approach God in prayer. Prayer is always *tefilla le'ani*, the call of the poor. This does not mean that the one who is not an *ani* dare not pray. Rather it indicates that we may all turn to God in prayer because each one of us stands before Him in the inescapable situation of his creaturely needfulness.

This is how the teachers of Judaism understood the words of the psalmist: "Hearer of prayer, to You all flesh will come" (Ps. 65:3). That God hears prayer has significance only because He is accessible to "all flesh" in the needfulness of its being. Rabbi Yehuda Bar Shalom explained this in the name of Rabbi Eleazar. A human being will not pay much attention to the words of a poor man, but he will listen to the rich or the mighty. With the Lord, it is not so. Women or slaves, the rich and the poor, they are alike before Him. One may learn it from the case of Moses. He was the master of all the prophets. Yet, it is said of him what is said of the *ani*. Of Moses it is said: "A prayer of Moses, the man of God. Lord, You have been our shelter in every generation" (Ps. 90:1); the same term is used of any poor soul, as we read: "A prayer for the lowly when they grow overwhelmed and pour out their lament before the Lord" (Ps. 102:1). "This is called prayer and that is called prayer, in order to teach you that all are alike in prayer before the ever-present One" (Exodus Rabba 21:4).

Needless to say, Moses, the man of God, did not pray like any poor afflicted person. His prayer must have reflected the greatness of his soul and the mightiness of his intellect. Yet, the outpouring of the heart of the lowliest of God's creatures is prayer and even the plea of a Moses is nothing more than prayer. We may pray not on account of what we are, but rather on account of what we lack. It is, therefore, not the spiritual quality of the good that we ask for which matters, not the philosophical depth of our thought nor the mystical surrender of our personal desires, but the intensity of the need, the depth of the misery alone out of which we call Him who is near because He is needed. One can pray only because God does not despise "a broken and oppressed heart." At best, the plea of the philosopher or the mystic will be prayer; but no more prayer than the cry that reaches God in the dead of night out of the dungeons of a soul along skid row. In fact, the philosopher who would pray to God only for the nobler things of life may easily be a pedantic bore, imagining that God might be impressed with his ethics but not with the hunger pangs of his poor ulcerated bowels. And how amused might God be – or perhaps, disgusted? – by the antics of the little mystic who would "ask of God as a gift God Himself," and would consider it below the dignity of his faith to settle for anything less, but yet would ask for the first prize in the religious lottery with the same greediness of the soul with which the next best yokel may hope for divine assistance in order to hit the jackpot in the Irish sweepstakes. It is unlikely that God could be moved by the one more than by the other. It is not our greatness – which counts for nothing in His eyes – that causes Him to make Himself accessible to human entreaty, but His fatherly compassion with the lowliness of our creaturely situation. A form of mystical communion with God may indeed be God's greatest gift to man. But man can live without the enjoyment of the glory of the Divine Presence; he cannot do without his needful sustenance. On account of that alone may he pray.

It is the need alone that God considers. We are all alike before Him in prayer, for the sorrow of the meanest of his creatures is no less a sorrow than that of the master among His prophets. In keeping with such insight, numerous are the suggestions in talmudic and midrashic literature that the prayer of the lowly ones may indeed be heard sooner by God than that of the greatest among men. The same Rabbi Shimon Bar Shalom, whose words I have quoted elsewhere, continues to make his point that in prayer God considers the need and not the person, by explaining what happened at the Red Sea. When Pharaoh approached, the children of Israel began to cry to God. But when Moses too started to pray, God said to him: "Why are you standing here praying? My children have already prayed, and I have heard their prayers." This, says Rabbi Bar Shalom, is implied in the meaning of the words which God addressed to Moses: "Why are you crying out to Me?" (Ex. 14:15). The phrase does sound somewhat brusque. What else could Moses have done at a moment of apparent hopelessness but pray? The midrashic interpreter seems to discern almost a rebuff to Moses and lets God stand as a father with his children on the one side and Moses, as if he were an outsider, on the other. And very likely, Moses, at this moment of supreme crisis in the history of the people, when everything so dearly gained seemed in jeopardy, was not one of them. For Moses was indeed so much greater than all of them. His faith, so much stronger than theirs; his conviction in the God-ordained destiny of Israel unshakable. He was so much closer to God's counsel than they were. However, just because of all that, he must have felt the crisis of the hour much less than the people. They were terror-stricken and, with the horror of impending annihilation in their hearts, they cried out to God. God heard the cry of His children, whose agony was indeed agony, rather than the prayer of Moses, who was not a child but the "man of God" and could take it all the better.

In quite a similar vein, however no longer interpreting a text but rather enacting the Jewish concept of prayer, the Talmud tells the story of how the sick son of Rabbi Yoḥanan ben Zakkai was helped by prayer. When everything seemed lost, Rabbi Yoḥanan ben Zakkai called in Rabbi Ḥanina ben Dosa and said to him: "Hanina, my son, ask for God's mercy for him that he may live." Rabbi Ḥanina prayed and the boy was healed. Then Rabbi Yoḥanan ben Zakkai said: Even if I had done so all day, I would not have been heard. Rabbi Yoḥanan was the head of the Sanhedrin, the greatest Jew of his generation. His wife could not suppress the question: "Is Ḥanina greater than you?" "No," answered Rabbi Yoḥanan, "but he is like a servant before the King, I am like a minister before the King" (Berakhot 34b). At times of prayer, the servant is closer to Him than the prince, because the servant's need is greater. Once, when in a time of drought Rabbi Ḥaggi ordered a public fast, they were answered with rain. Said the Rabbi: Not because I deserve it, but because it is written, "For He has not spurned or scorned the suffering of the lowly" (Ps. 22:25).

In its original form, prayer is not asking God for anything; it is not a request. It is a cry; an elementary outburst of woe, a spontaneous call in need; a hurt, a sorrow, given voice. It is the call of human helplessness directed to God. It is not asking, but coming with one's burden before God. It is like the child's running to the mother because it hurts. It is not the bandage that the child seeks instinctively but the nearness of the mother, to unburden his heart to the one of whose love he is certain. So the human being brings his sorrow before God: look, O God, what has been done to me, consider what has become of me. This is the essence of prayer. Only children can pray like this or – *tzaddikim*, the men of great faith who in the depth of their piety have gained a new childlike trust in God. Interpreting the words of the psalmist, "I will pour out my lament before Him, tell my troubles to Him" (Ps. 142:3), the Midrash remarks: "Thus the men of faith declare their troubles before God."

In all their simplicity, these few words, which seem to add nothing to the text, are among the deepest observations on the essence of prayer. To pour out one's heart before God means simply to tell God about one's troubles. To pray means to make God the confidant of one's sorrow and need. The asking and begging are natural enough, but they are of secondary importance. Decisive is the pouring of the heart because one has to; the pouring out of the heart before God because He is the nearest, because He is the closest, because He is the natural confidant of the human soul. All asking is in reality self-seeking; whether we ask for bread or health, for the power to do good, or "the enjoyment of God," we are asking for ourselves, for the things that we desire. "Give, give!" is no prayer, no matter what we ask for. We may ask only if we pray, if we cry with the need of the creature; if the request comes without premeditation in the wake of the cry. Our asking may have the quality of prayer, if it issues from the act of intimacy, of having made God our confidant.

In writings about prayer, one often comes across the question: What need is there to ask God for anything? Surely He is omniscient, He knows all about us. Does He have to be informed about our troubles? It is, of course, no solution to the problem to limit one's prayers to just a few basic requests. If prayer is nothing more than a memo to the Almighty regarding our daily requirements, it is mere foolishness, no matter how fundamental to our very existence those requirements are. On the other hand, if prayer is not just asking and informing God concerning our needs, one cannot limit it solely because God in His omniscience knows it all. Of course God knows it all. Judaism even affirms that there are prayers which are heard without ever being uttered and that are answered as one is about to speak them. How could it be otherwise in a religion steeped in the tradition of an Isaiah, who taught his people that "before they call out to Me, I shall answer – while they are yet speaking, I shall respond" (Is. 65:24). The teachers of the Midrash knew how to weave the aspect of God's omniscience into a deepening of the meaning of prayer. The words of the psalm, "Even before a word is on my tongue, You, Lord, know it all" (Ps. 139:4), are explained by the Midrash, in the context in which they occur, in the following manner:

> Thus spoke David before the Lord: You know when I rest and when I rise. And not only that, but every step that I shall ever make is already revealed to You; and not only from now on, but it has been known to You even ever before I came into this world… This is meant by the phrase "Even before a word is on my tongue"; there is no song, no psalm, not a prayer, which I shall ever utter which is not already known to You. (*Midrash Tehillim* 139:3)

Yet, such a declaration too is prayer. To come before God and to say to Him: "You know it all, you know it even better than I do," and then to pour out one's heart before Him, may be among the greatest of prayers. With its incomparable ability to hear the finest nuances of the

Hebrew text, the Midrash interprets the words of the psalmist, "Give ear to my words, Lord; understand my reflections" (Ps. 5:2), as referring to two different forms of prayer: the one uttered in words, the other silently embedded in the heart. Elaborating the phrase of the psalm, it is explained: "David prayed to God: Creator of the universe! When I have the strength to stand before You in prayer and to utter my words, do listen; but when I am without strength, You consider what is in my heart, understand my reflections" (*Midrash Tehillim* 5:2). For reasons that we shall discuss later, one should pray in a synagogue. But Rabbi Eliezer ben Yaakov, one of the great *Tanna'im,* taught: "If you cannot go to the synagogue, pray in your field; if you cannot pray in the field, pray in your house; if you cannot pray in your house, pray on your bed; and if you are unable to do that either, meditate in your heart, as it is written: 'Speak in your heart upon your bed, and be still' (Ps. 4:5)." To dwell in silence before God may also be praying, for the root of prayer is neither informing God, nor asking Him; but, in intimate reliance on Him, making him the confidant of our heart.

How long should a prayer be? There are differences of opinion on this between the teachers of the Talmud (Berakhot 21b), as there may well be. However, the opinion of Rabbi Yoḥanan has become the accepted halakha, according to which, "Would that man prayed all day." Indeed, who would wish to limit the outpourings of an afflicted soul! Shall we say to a man: Don't bother the Almighty; He is perfectly well informed about your plight! One might as well upbraid a child, seeking the comforting arms of the mother, since she knows all about the child's troubles and need not be informed. We pray because we have to pour out our hearts to the One who knows all. Yes, we do it, *because* He knows all and understands all. If He were not omniscient, we would not come before Him so free of all shyness in the needfulness of our nature.

Because it is only on account of the needfulness of our humanity that we may pray, there is no creaturely need out of which we dare not call God. Be it the body or the soul, the affliction of the individual or the group, of man or mankind, in prayer we tumble into the presence of God with our load. Thus, even prayers for vengeance, which at first glance rightly scandalize us, may be genuine prayers; and more so than the noblest literary exercises composed by philosophers in the peace of their study and in accordance with the ultimate principles of some ethical theory. A greater man of prayer than the prophet Jeremiah one can hardly conceive. Yet, he did supplicate in the words:

> The Lord of Hosts discerns who is righteous.
> He sees into both heart and mind.
> I will yet witness Your revenge upon them,
> for to You I have disclosed my disputes. (Jer. 20:12)

Now, such a prayer, incorporated in a planned service in a synagogue that begins at 9:00 a.m., and has to be over by 11:00 a.m., one to which people get dressed up in their Sabbath-best fully conscious that they are doing what is only right and proper, such a prayer introduced at what we have come to call a divine service, would indeed be an abomination. But to compare our way of praying with that of a Jeremiah would be a sacrilege committed against the prophet.

Those words of Jeremiah are indeed terrible words, but prayer may be terrible and yet be prayer and, perhaps, even more prayer on account of the terror that breathes in it. Not what the prophet asks for makes his words prayer, but that they are the creaturely cry of a greatly afflicted soul, of a man hunted and persecuted for going about the business of God, a mission moreover for which he has not asked but which – very much against his will – was imposed upon him by God. Those words are prayer because they were uttered by Jeremiah, the man whose life experience was summed up when he poured out his heart:

> Cursed be the day that I was born.
> May the day that my mother gave birth to me not be blessed.
> Cursed be the man who informed my father,
> saying, "A son was born to you."
> He caused him so much joy.
> May that man be like the cities
> that the Lord overturned without regret.

May he hear shrieking each morning
and sobbing in the afternoon.
He should have killed me as I left the womb.
Then my mother would have been my grave
and her womb forever pregnant.
Why did I leave the womb
to see only misery and agony?
My days have ended in shame. (Jer. 20:14–18)

Those words of the prophet are prayer because they are the elementary utterance of a life of "labor and sorrow" which made the prophet turn to the only one to whom he could turn with the exclamation at the end of which his cry for vengeance is found:

You persuaded me, Lord,
and I let myself be persuaded.
You overpowered me,
and You prevailed.
I have become a laughingstock all day long:
they all mock me.
For whenever I speak prophecy, I shout;
I call out, Injustice! Violence!
The Lord's word has brought upon me
derision and scorn all day long.
I said to myself: I will not make mention of it.
I will no longer speak in His name.
But it resides within me like a flaming fire,
locked into my bones.
I wearied of holding it back. I could not.
I have overheard the slanderous whispers,
a terror all around:
"Testify and let us testify."
All of my trusted friends
await my collapse. They say,
"Perhaps we can entrap him, overcome him,
and thereby take our revenge upon him."

> But the Lord is with me like a mighty warrior.
> Therefore my pursuers will stumble and not prevail.
> They will suffer great shame and not succeed,
> an eternal disgrace, never to be forgotten. (Jer. 20:7–11)

All this is prayer because it is human agony turned God-ward.

This may be the place to say a few words on the Jewish attitude toward prayer for one's enemy. The intention of praying for one's enemy is indeed admirable; its execution, however, is mostly so problematic that one wonders whether it would not be a sign of far greater charity toward an enemy if one overcame the temptation of such noble intentions. This kind of prayer is not only philosophically and theologically problematic but also ethically questionable. How can one pray for anyone else at all? Do we mean to remind God of his existence and to prevail upon God to take pity on him? But as we saw, the request is not the essence of prayer. Prayer is the need that cries out to God and that may issue into a request. But a request without need, especially if it is made on behalf of someone else, is sheer impudence before God. The one for whom we "pray," is he not also a child of God? Is God neglectful of His children? Does God require my intercession in order to be induced to have pity on His own children? The rebuff that such prayer deserves might be infinitely more appropriate than the one which, as we saw earlier in this chapter, was administered to Moses for thinking that it was up to him to pray for God's children.

One may pray for another person if one can cry to God with his need; if one can identify oneself with his sorrow. Without such identification, one does not pray, one only asks. One dares pray for an enemy only if one has succeeded in overcoming all sense of enmity toward him and if, in addition, one is able to feel the agony of his soul as if it were one's own. So much so that one must pour out one's heart before God in order to unburden oneself of the misery of our fellow man. Without such complete inner reconciliation and identification with an enemy, one does not pray, one only flatters oneself with the nobility of one's own sentiments. However, if one stands before God with "the proud consciousness of those who have apprehended the right faith,"[1] praying that He may redeem the heathens and the infidels from their deviltry and wickedness, as He has already redeemed oneself from all such evil, that He may grant them as much light and truth as one has oneself already received, that God may elevate them from their condition of shame to the glory of one's own position, then prayer has been distorted out of all recognition.

"There is no elevation before the All-Present" (Berakhot 10b) is the principle that determines the Jewish attitude in prayer. Standing before God, one dare not adopt an attitude of pride or any form of self-exaltation; one can only pray from a position of creaturely lowliness. How then can one pray for an enemy? If one cannot identify oneself with his misery, as indeed most people are unable to do, how can one pray for him without casting reflection on oneself, without praying in self-righteousness and conceit? One can pray for an enemy only if one is able to find a position of need that one shares with him. One may pray for him out of a situation of a common need of men.

How this is to be done, Jews were taught many, many centuries ago by their teachers in the Talmud. It is told of Rabbi Meir that some outlaws who lived in his neighborhood subjected him to a great deal of suffering. In his despair, Rabbi Meir prayed to God that they may die. His wife, Beruria, reproached him with the words "Do you think this is the way of getting rid of sinners? The psalmist does not say, 'Let sinners vanish from the earth' (Ps. 104:35),[2] but, 'let sins cease from the earth.' And consider now the end of the verse, which runs: 'And the wicked be no more.' If sins cease, there will be no wickedness anymore. Pray then that they may return to God. Rabbi Meir prayed and the outlaws returned to God" (Berakhot 10a). Rabbi Meir cried out in a situation of personal helplessness. When he prayed rightly, he supplicated that sins may disappear and that his fellow men may return to God. However, there has never lived a Jew who was not himself in need of the same

1. See Heiler, *Prayer*, 551.
2. Beruria's interpretation of the verse is closer to the literary meaning of the Hebrew original than the one usually adopted by translators.

prayer. The more he was a Jew, the more he realized his own need for return. To be cleansed of one's sins and to return to God is a continuous, ever-present requirement for all men. Rabbi Eliezer, who lived a generation before Rabbi Meir, on his deathbed bequeathed it as a spiritual legacy to his disciples that the effort to return to God must be the lifelong religious responsibility of man (Shabbat 137b). Praying that his enemies may return to God, Rabbi Meir prayed from a situation of a critical urgency which he shared with them.

Spontaneous Prayer and the Service of the Heart

Thus far, I have discussed prayer in a specific sense, as an expression of human need and as supplication. There are, of course, also prayers of praise and thanksgiving. Moved by the majesty of God's creation, the psalmist exclaimed: "The heavens tell of God's glory" (Ps. 19:2). One may also praise Him for His mercies shown to people or for His law which He gave to man. It is equally natural to thank Him for help and protection. Jewish praying is inconceivable without the sentiments "Thank the Lord for He is good – His loving-kindness is forever" (Ps. 136:1).

Jewish prayer is divided into three main categories: *shevaḥ, taḥanunim, hodaa* – hymns or praises, supplication, and thanksgiving. Although they are rather different in inspiration and content, they have one thing in common: in their origins, they are spontaneous reactions of the religious spirit to certain types of human experience. Praise and thanksgiving may be as spontaneous as the outpouring of the heart in supplication. Confronted with the grandeur of God's handiwork, one may be overcome with a sense of awe and elation which might seek expression before God with no less force than an experience of grief or sorrow. And having actually been granted His salvation, one may have the urge to thank Him with no less fervor than when one was first moved to implore Him in the hour of one's trial and visitation. The three types of prayer have then in common the fact that they are occasional prayers; they are man's response to occasional experiences. That prayer constitutes such a response to momentary experience makes it, in its original form, free and most intimately personal.

It is easy to acknowledge the religious importance of the spontaneity of free personal prayer. It is unparalleled in intensity of emotion and sincerity of devotion. Yet, such immediate and free praying, brought on by specific occasions, has its pitfalls and shortcomings. In the case of supplication, this is quite obvious. That a human being, in a situation of crisis, should seek the nearness of God is understandable enough. That he should seek it only in such a situation is also understandable, but not necessarily right in the context of a broader God-oriented interpretation of human existence. To seek God only in a time of trouble implies that one needs Him only when in trouble. The free outpouring of the heart may indeed be felt very deeply but, however genuine, it is a crisis prayer. God, however, is not just a Crisis God.

Once again, the midrashic teacher directs our attention to a proper understanding of the issue involved. The sixty-third psalm commences with the words: "A Psalm of David, when he was in the wilderness of Yehuda." With surprising boldness, the Midrash comments: "The case of David exemplifies the words of Isaiah, who says: 'Lord – in anguish they came to You, pouring out whispers to You even as You beat them.' When does Israel seek the Lord? In time of their trouble! As it is written, 'In my distress I called to the Lord'... Here, too, 'when he was in the wilderness of Yehuda'; 'A psalm of David in his kingship' is a phrase we do not find, but we do find, 'A psalm of David when he was in the wilderness'" (*Midrash Tehillim* 63:1). Turning to God spontaneously in time of trouble may cast a reflection on the value of such prayer, if it represents a small island of God-seeking in the midst of an ocean of God-forgetting. That such was not the case with King David we appreciate if we read the very same sixty-third psalm whose introductory words served as a basis for the midrashic comment we have quoted. Let us consider that psalm:

O God,
You are my God;
I seek You desperately.
My soul thirsts for You;
my flesh longs for You
in a parched and weary land
that has no water…
Your loving-kindness is better than life,
so my lips praise You,
so I will bless You as long as I live,
as I lift up my hands in Your name.
My soul will be nourished as with a rich feast;
my mouth will sing praises with joyful lips.
I think of You upon my bed;
I contemplate You in the vigil of night.

David finds himself in the wilderness, in a weary and dry land. There is no water or much vegetation. David is thirsty and hungry, perhaps even in danger of his life. Especially at night, one must be on the watch. It is a situation of crisis, an experience of great trouble. David turns to God, making Him the confidant of his tribulations. At this moment, what becomes of all his needs? The tortures of thirst are superseded by the soul's thirst for God; the hunger of the body is felt as a longing of the flesh for God. The dangers to his life are dismissed because God's loving-kindness is better than life. The leanness of the land is a reminder of the "rich feast" with which his soul is satisfied. And as to the disconcerting night vigils in the solitude of the desert, they are welcome occasions for meditation on God. The psalm is a free personal response to a specific experience of trouble; but a response in which the momentary urgency of human needs is transformed into the ever-present urgency of man's need for God.

What is normally considered the realities of a given human situation become a mere symbol of the overriding reality of all human situations, i.e., man's dependence on God. Those who can pray as King David may escape the pitfalls of occasional prayer. Most people, however, do not have the genius of prayer of the psalmist. With them, the very intensity of experience, and the free response to it in prayer, may boomerang into a form of self-seeking. Those who remember God only in their troubles are concerned only with themselves. Neither are hymns and thanksgiving prayers free from the problematic aspect of spontaneity. When, because of a momentary realization of the majestic manifestation of the Divine Presence, man's lips part in adoring acknowledgment, may it not also imply a limiting of the glory of God to the moment and the occasion, as if the rest of space and time were empty of it? The question applies in a similar sense to spontaneous prayers of thanksgiving as well. If thanksgiving is rendered solely when the sentiments of the individual are inspired by the actual experience of having received God's bounty, on this or that specific occasion, does it not also suggest that for all other occasions there is no reason to thank God?

The truth, of course, is that every moment of life is an occasion for praising God, for all the time the earth is filled with His glory, all the time man is in the presence of His glory. Thus all life is one continuous occasion for thanksgiving, for God's mercies and wonders are always with us. And if supplication means turning to God in one's need, man is never without his creaturely needfulness; his need is not occasion-conditioned but existential. Man is never without it, and, therefore, he is never without the need of turning to God in creaturely dependence. There is no time in human life which is not an occasion for prayer. This is the deeper significance of the saying of Rabbi Yoḥanan, which I have quoted in the previous chapter: "Would that man prayed all day" (Berakhot 10a). If Rabbi Yoḥanan speaks specifically of supplication, his remark should be completed by the statement of Rabbi Levi, made in the name of Rabbi Ḥanina, which applies to both thanksgiving and hymnal prayer. He declared: "One should praise God for every breath that one takes" (Genesis Rabba 14:11). Meditating on the physiological function of breathing, one has reason to praise the Maker; being able to breathe, one may thank Him all the moments of one's life.

In view of the ever-present appropriateness of prayer, free occasional prayer becomes problematic. But can one pray all day, all of one's life? And since, obviously, this is impossible, how is the dilemma to be resolved? In Judaism, it is done by means of the institution of obligatory prayer. There are times set aside for prayer: morning, afternoon, and evening. There are prescribed, ever-recurring occasions for prayer, praise, and thanksgiving. Beside the free spontaneous prayer of the specific occasion stands the *tefillat ḥova,* the obligatory prayer of the normal routine of life. The obligatory prayer, which rhythmically accompanies the way of the Jew through life, gives acknowledgment to the threefold truth – that there is an ever-present occasion for praising God; that man's needfulness and dependence on God are perennially inherent in his situation; that he is ceaselessly bound in gratitude to the Creator. The Jew prays regularly because one ought to pray all the time but cannot do so. One may also say that in free personal prayer, man responds to the events which are contingent on his own specific situation; in obligatory prayer man relates his experience to the essential nature of the human situation. Far from abolishing it, *tefillat ḥova,* obligatory prayer, makes *tefillat reshut,* free prayer, acceptable. Once we give expression, through obligatory prayer, to man's unceasing need to pray, the individual may lose himself freely in the spontaneity of occasion-conditioned praying, without suggesting that what one seeks and affirms occasionally has only occasional validity.

Only because of *tefillat ḥova* does the Talmud refer to prayer as *avoda shebalev,* service of the heart (Taanit 2a). When a man, overwhelmed by the impact of a specific experience, seeks the nearness of God or bursts forth in *halleluya* or bows down in gratitude, it is prayer but not service of God yet; it is a human response to a potent stimulus. But when he prays without the stimulus of a specific occasion, acknowledging that man is always dependent on God, that independently of all personal experience God is always to be praised and to be thanked, then – and only then – is prayer divine service of the heart. It is noteworthy that, whereas Judaism is life under the law of God, the halakha casts a somewhat ambiguous light on obligatory prayer. Most of the authorities maintain that the obligation to pray is not a biblical law but was instituted by the Rabbis. Maimonides seems to stand alone in his opinion that prayer is prescribed by the Bible. However, even according to him, the times of prayer, the number of prayers or their nature and content, were left to be determined by man. It would seem to us that the ambiguity of the place that prayer has acquired in the system of the halakha reflects its essential quality. Prayer in its original free and personal form cannot be obligatory. No law can be imposed on the outpouring of the heart. The heart prays when and in the way it must because of its own inner necessity. But such praying has its problematic aspects. In order to remove them, it calls for obligatory prayer. Obligatory prayer emerges out of the inadequacies of spontaneous prayer. It is an obligation which arises out of a human activity that represents a vital manifestation of religious living but which yet cannot be prescribed. Prayer, which is always of the heart or else it is not prayer, calls for the service of the heart.

The Art of Praying

The pitfalls of personal prayer, which I have discussed and which necessitate man to move on from the outpouring to the service of the heart, show that praying has to be learned. Naive, childlike praying may be extremely moving, but most people are not as simple as the ignorant country boy who blew his little whistle in the *Beit HaMidrash* of the Baal Shem and made things so much easier for the Master on a Yom Kippur. Nor do we have the purity of the *tzaddikim,* who know instinctively how to make God their confidant. We certainly do not have the gigantic spiritual powers of the psalmist that would transform an acute crisis of life in the wilderness into the symbolism of man's existential dependence on God and only on God. We have to learn how to pray. There is a relationship between the right kind of praying and human understanding. At the head of our requests. which are incorporated in the *Shemoneh Esreh,* stands the one for understanding. According to the Talmud Yerushalmi, Rabbi Yehuda HaNasi was surprised that the prayer for understanding was not recited on the Sabbath. He remarked: "If there is no understanding, whence prayer?" (Y. Berakhot 5:2). Spontaneous prayer is, on the whole, free from rules and regulations. In Judaism, it is with the help of obligatory prayer that we learn how to pray in all situations.

The prototype of all prayer is the *Shemoneh Esreh,* which in the Talmud is referred to by the general term of *tefilla.* It is the prescribed prayer of Judaism. It is constructed in accordance with the principle, put in words by Rabbi Simlai: "One should begin with the praises of God and only after them should one proceed with intercession" (Berakhot 32a). After the intercession follows thanksgiving. So that the pattern of obligatory prayer is: *shevaḥ, bakasha, hodaa* – praise, supplication, thanksgiving. Nevertheless, it is important to realize that the rule for obligatory prayer is derived from the free and spontaneous prayers of a Moses, a David, and a Solomon. This is how one ought to pray, since this is how great religious personalities pray freely. The obligatory Jewish prayer is framed in the image of the exemplary personal prayer of great Jews.

What is the significance of the order of praise, supplication, and thanksgiving? It is easy to misunderstand this order as if it suggested that one ingratiate oneself with the Almighty before making a request and that, in order to inveigle Him into the granting of the request, one thanks Him in conclusion as if He had already granted it.[1] Flattery is no prayer. Anything but strictest honesty of thought and sentiment is inconceivable before God. In the Talmud one finds a remarkable explanation of the term *Anshei Knesset HaGedola,* the Men of the Great Synagogue. It is said that the masters who established the text of the *Shemoneh Esreh* earned for themselves that title of honor because "they restored the crown to its old dignity." Moses called God *HaKel, hagadol, hagibbor, vehanora,* "the great, mighty and awesome God." Came along Jeremiah and he wondered: "Idolators are cackling in His sanctuary, where is His awesomeness?" He stopped saying, "awesome." Then came Daniel and exclaimed: "Idolators oppress His children, where is His mightiness?" He did not say, "mighty." Then, the men of the Great Synagogue came along and explained: On the contrary! Such is His mightiness that He controls His anger and is long-suffering with the wicked; and this is His

1. One might easily misunderstand the statement of Rabbi Ḥanina, for instance, in Berakhot 32a. A careful reading of the text, however, should indicate that Rabbi Ḥanina does not explain the reason for the sequence of the sections, but the nature of each section by itself.

awesomeness, for were it not for the fear of Him, how could a single nation survive among all the heathens. Thus, they reintroduced the original phraseology of Moses into Jewish prayer. But how to understand the audacity of Jeremiah and Daniel in uprooting a form of invocation that was established by Moses himself? Rabbi Eleazar says in answer: "Knowing that God was truthful, they would not lie to Him" (Yoma 69b). In the eyes of Jewish tradition the dropping of a phrase of invocation that was used by Moses was an act of impiety toward the master of all prophets of which particularly such outstanding personalities as Jeremiah and Daniel should not be guilty. Yet, it was found justified because one dare not stand before God with insincerity in one's heart. One must come to God in truth. We must mean what we say. How else can one approach God, who knows the innermost recesses of the human heart?

What then is the significance of the trilogy in the *Shemoneh Esreh*? We have to recall what I have said about the problems of occasional prayer. In it, one remembers God only in a time of trouble. But independently of any specific experience, man is existentially in need of God. This is acknowledged by the regularity of obligatory prayer. However, by the shift from the specific occasion to the human situation as such, we gain a different starting point for our praying. He who approaches God under the impact of a contingent experience begins with himself and with what has happened to him. In obligatory prayer, one does not start from a personal crisis situation; one begins with man's essential nature, realizing that it is constituted in the fact that man is God's creature. Free of the urgency of an immediate experience, in obligatory prayer one does not approach God with what life has done to one, but with the knowledge of what God means to man. Thus, it becomes logical to commence with God, to acknowledge Him with our praises before we approach in our needful humanity. Laboring under the pressure of a momentary crisis, even in prayer man is often self-centered and preoccupied with himself. In obligatory prayer, one begins with preoccupation with God; one turns to Him not because of what hurts man, but because of what He is to man and His creation.

As the starting point is different, so also does the nature of the supplication in obligatory prayer show a character of its own. Earlier in our discussion we saw that the outpouring of the heart was basically an elementary cry in a moment of crisis, which imperceptibly changes into supplication. The service of the heart, on the other hand, is lacking this sense of peril which begets the cry. The request here is not carried by spontaneity born of anxiety or agony. The supplication is, as it were, premeditated. Is it then nothing but give-give prayer?

Obligatory prayer in Judaism has a *matbe'a shetavu ḥakhamim*, "a coinage minted by the Sages." It is this coinage that reveals its meaning. One may find its significance incorporated in a comment which the Midrash connected with the words of the psalmist: *emunim notzer Hashem*, "the Lord protects the faithful" (Ps. 31:24). Playing on the etymological association between *emuna* and *amen*, the Midrash interprets the word "faithful" as meaning those who in faith answer with Amen at the end of each paragraph in the *Shemoneh Esreh*. "They hear the reader recite, 'Blessed are You, Lord, who revives the dead,' and in faith they affirm, 'Amen.' With all their might, they believe that the Lord is the reviver of the dead, even though the resurrection of the dead has not yet been witnessed. They call Him the Redeemer of Israel, yet they are not redeemed. They say, 'Blessed are You, the Builder of Jerusalem,' but she is not yet rebuilt. Notwithstanding their experience, they affirm with the power of faith that God is the Redeemer of Israel and the Builder of Jerusalem" (*Midrash Tehillim* 31:5).

This then is the nature of our supplication. We ask God for understanding and, independently of what has been granted to us of wisdom and insight, we praise Him as being the granter of wisdom. We implore Him to bring us near to Him and to forgive us our sins, but while we are still far removed from Him, we praise Him as the One who causes His people to return to Him and forgives them their sins. Because of our lot, we beseech Him to redeem us, but even though unredeemed, we exalt Him as our Redeemer. In the midst of our exile, we acknowledge Him as the One who gathers in the scattered remnants of His people Israel. Because of the plight of "the righteous and the pious" in the present condition of the world, we approach Him in prayer that His mercies may be stirred toward them.

But even though our prayers are as yet far from being fulfilled, we laud Him as the stay and sure support of the righteous. In the midst of the ruins of Jerusalem, praying for the holy city, we worship Him as the Builder of Jerusalem. We pray and ask; but as we are praying, we acknowledge God as if He had already granted our prayer. We come before Him with our needs; but as we supplicate Him, we call on Him as if our needs had already been met. This is the true nature of the service of the heart. One asks, but in such a way that one transforms one's need into an affirmation of faith in God. Nor does this faith mean that we believe that God will do exactly as we implore Him to do. No matter how He may respond to our prayer, He is God "who listens to prayer." No matter what our own destiny may be, He is the Forgiver, the Healer, the Redeemer, He is the One who blesses the land and the fruit thereof. This is not mere asking. In such prayer we declare our continuous dependence on God for everything and, independently of all personal experience – and in the very teeth of any apparent proof to the contrary – affirm our faith in His ever-present providence. Asking, we acknowledge our dependence on God for our very being and affirm our faith in Him as if our needs had already been satisfied.

In the spontaneous, crisis prayer, the need of the moment brings us before God. It is the cry that justifies the request. In the obligatory prayer, the request is justified as an exercise in faith. This is perhaps the reason why even the pitch of the voice is regulated in obligatory prayer. One should recite the *Shemoneh Esreh* silently. According to talmudic preaching, "he who raises his voice in prayer is of the people of little faith" (Berakhot 24b). No such dictum has ever been applied to free personal prayer. Where the releasing stimulus is fear and anxiety, the raising of the voice, the cry, is natural. Where, however, the essence of praying is the affirmation of one's faith in the providence of God on whom man so completely depends and relies, any sign of anxiety reflects on the depth of the affirmation.

We may now cast another glance at the two questions which I discussed in the chapter "Prayer and the Needs of Man," in connection with the original form of prayer. They are found to be completely groundless in the light of the obligatory prayer of Judaism. Since the requests take on the form of divine service, acknowledging our dependence on and our faith in God, needless to say that in prayer we do not inform God of our needs, which would of course be utterly meaningless. Though all our needs are before Him, we yet pray because in prayer, we worship Him by way of our needfulness. Similarly, not only do we pray for *all* the needs of our life, but within the meaning of obligatory prayer, it would be improper not to do so. Since prayer is acknowledgment of man's creaturely dependence on his Creator, it is right to acknowledge it completely, even as regards our most insignificant needs. Since prayer is affirmation of faith in divine providence, it would be like an insult to God to exempt from such affirmation any aspect of our dependent humanity. Paraphrasing a familiar talmudic statement, it is correct to say that God's providence reaches from the highest to the lowest: the highest among His creatures cannot do without it, and the lowest among them are not excluded from it; the lowliest of our needs are as little neglected by Him as the most noble ones (Avoda Zara 3b).

It may now be worth comparing the relationship in which the three types of prayer stand to each other in free prayer, to the one in which they stand in the context of obligatory prayer. As we have seen, in personal prayer it is always a specific experience that calls forth the praying response. Overwhelmed by awe and admiration, one worships; at the moment of crisis, one supplicates; having received God's bounties, one thanks. Each occasion is different from the other; each type of prayer is unlike the other. The three categories remain unrelated responses to unrelated experiences. In obligatory prayer, the middle section of supplication is the natural passage from praise to thanksgiving. In spontaneous entreaty, the need is all-important; in obligatory prayer, the need is transformed by an act of faith. One requests; yet, requesting, one worships. The supplication in the obligatory prayer in Judaism is rather like a specific version of praise. Significantly, the intercessions of the *Shemoneh Esreh*, though they are *bakashot*, entreaties, are usually referred to as *berakhot*, blessings of God by man. "Blessed are You who heals the sick," is not a request, but a praise. It is appropriate to conclude such praying with thanksgiving. Having asked as if we had already received, we proceed to thank because we have indeed received. Because God is forever the Healer, ever the Redeemer, ever the Provider, man is ever the recipient of His mercies. For the Jew, man's dependence on God means that at every moment he looks to the future with faith in God's providence and to the past, with gratitude for it.

The relationship between the three sections, however, is not only one of sequence but also one of interpenetration. Each section takes cognizance of the other two and shows the signs of their influence. This follows from the viewpoint of obligatory prayer. As we have seen, obligatory prayer does not recognize specific occasions; for it, all occasions are alike. Every moment of life presents an occasion to praise, to supplicate, and to thank, as well. As we supplicate, so have we reason to praise and to thank; and as we thank, so have we reason to supplicate and to praise. Every aspect of man's relationship to God is wedded inseparably to every other aspect. The praising man ought to be also the supplicating man and the thanking man at the same time. The threefold significance of every moment of human existence has shaped the nature of Jewish supplication. Our request becomes an affirmation of faith; the moment of supplication being identical with that of praise and thanksgiving. And since he who asks under the power of his affirmation in faith asks as if he had already received, our request is on the verge of turning into thanksgiving.

As we conclude our plea for redemption with blessing God as the Redeemer, we are only a very small step removed from thanking Him for redeeming us. Supplication so submitted is not only a specific form of praise, but also an anticipation of thanksgiving. However, as supplication is related to the other two categories of prayer, so in turn is each of the other two related to the rest. The praise that we offer is not a paean to the Infinite, but to the God of history, who acts for the sake of His creation. We praise Him as the God of the *Avot,* who is great and mighty and awesome, yet also the intimate God of the fathers, rendering loving-kindness to all, a king who is Helper, Savior, and Shield. We exalt Him for His *gevurot,* His might. He is mighty forever, mighty to save and sustain the living in His love and great mercy. He is infinitely mighty and uses His power to support the falling, to heal the sick, to free the captive. We praise God, who is near to His creation, and on whom each of His creatures depends. We praise Him out of our finitude and dependence. How close is such praise to supplication, especially to the supplication of trust in God, who is thus praiseworthy! We praise Him out of our situation of ever-present need of Him. Even when we extol Him for His holiness, we do so mentioning the holy ones who bless Him daily. But the holy ones are holy because He is holy. We praise Him for His holiness that is the source of all sanctity among His creatures and in His creation. We praise Him, who notwithstanding His transcendence is so near because He is so needed. Such praise is almost interchangeable with thanksgiving.

As to the thanksgiving prayer itself, we do not thank for a specific blessing but for God's miracles that are with us every day and for His benefits that we receive at all times, "evening, morning, and noon." We thank Him, for He is "the Good One whose mercy never ceases," because He is "the Merciful One whose loving-kindness never ends." Here, thanksgiving has obviously become only another version of praise. However, just as supplication anticipates thanksgiving, so does thanksgiving hint at supplication. Since thanksgiving here is not a spontaneous response to a unique experience of having dramatically received a divine blessing but is tied to the normal routine of our everyday existence, how does one know that there is really occasion for giving thanks? How do we know of the miracles and benefits of God which are always with us? The Jewish answer is that one knows it because one lives, because man's dependence on God is such that one could not live for one moment without the goodness and mercy of God. We thank because we realize in the needfulness of our nature that we could not exist for a single breath without the Merciful One whose loving-kindness never ceases. Since every moment of man's life is a threefold occasion, for praise, supplication, and thanksgiving, the three types of prayer have been woven into one pattern. The theme of each one of them becomes meaningful in the context of the other two. We praise, almost thanking, with a hint of supplication; we supplicate and yet worship with anticipation of thanksgiving; we thank with praises for being sustained ceaselessly.

The Individual and the Community in Prayer

Perhaps the most significant feature of obligatory prayer as compared with free prayer is that *tefillat ḥova* is also *tefillat tzibbur*, that obligatory prayer is community prayer. Free prayer is always individual prayer, even when practiced in a congregational assembly. It is free because it is released by a specific experience and all specific experiences are most intimately individual. Only in the rarest of circumstances will a group undergo an experience as a group. In most cases, the same event will affect each one of the group individually; it will have its unique connotation in relationship to the life of each individual. Thus, the prayerful response to the experience will be an individual prayer. Obligatory prayer, being independent of any contingent individual occasion, is based on the existential situation of the Jew in relationship to God. It is not the prayer of one Jew in one situation; it is the prayer for all Jews at all times. Therefore, even when prayed by an individual in solitude, it remains in its essence communal prayer.[1]

1. In Talmud and Midrash, as well as in the codes, the term *tefillat tzibbur* is normally used to indicate prayer in community assembly. I shall yet have occasion to refer to

However, why do we speak of the existential situation of the Jew? Is there such a thing at all? Why is such praying Jewish? The acknowledgment of God's continuous presence for man, man's existential dependence on God and God's unceasing providence, the core of obligatory prayer, are universal concepts. Prayer based on them ought to be universal and not specifically Jewish. The answer to such questioning is that while obligatory prayer does incorporate universal ideas, the ideas are the crystallization of man's history with God. We saw in the first chapter, prayer means standing in the presence of God and one may confront only a personal God. Now, the personal God may be the subject of a certain type of philosophy or theology, but no mere philosophy or theology can give us such a God. The personal God one may know only from His revelations, from His manifestations in the life of individuals or peoples. History is the foundation of all praying. Already in the earliest part of our study, discussing the most intimately personal aspect of prayer, the outpouring of the heart, we had to link up with the historic experience of the community in order to resolve the dilemma of the confrontation. We saw how out of the depth of his being personally forsaken by God, the individual Jew may yet call God as if he confronted the Divine Presence, because he is sustained all the time, and in the teeth of his personal history, by the historic experience of Israel of the ever-present God.

The Jew may pray significantly on the spur of the moment because he is sustained by the Jewish awareness of the Divine Presence through the ages. It is the same corporate experience of all Israel that makes it possible for the Jew to formulate conceptually those universal principles which are incorporated in obligatory prayer. That God is forever present for man, that man is ever dependent on Him and ever sustained by Him, we cannot derive from any theology or philosophy, nor can we know it from a merely individual history. Jews know it on the strength of Israel's life with God. Only on the basis of the corporate history of the Jewish people can a Jew, notwithstanding all individual and momentary experience to the contrary, meaningfully affirm that God is Provider,

it in this specific sense. Here, however, I use the term in an attempt to determine an essential quality of obligatory prayer.

Healer, Redeemer, and Shield. Only because of that history does a Jew know that His mercies and loving-kindness are without an end, only on the strength of it can a Jew praise Him who is mighty to save. One cannot take one's stand on a theology and pray; one can only pray in the historic context of one's life with God. The purely individual history is necessary, it does not provide prayer with depth of emotion, but it is inadequate. Obligatory prayer is required to meet the inadequacies of free praying. The historic experience on which alone obligatory prayer could be founded had to be that of the Jewish people.

The most familiar meaning of the term *tefillat tzibbur*, community prayer, is the one which we find in talmudic and halakhic literature. It is praying together with the community. According to tradition, the prescribed services ought to be performed in communal assembly.[2] Individual prayer is usually practiced in solitude. Being alone with the Alone is usually considered most conducive to fervor and intensity in praying. Some of the greatest prayers have undoubtedly been articulated by lonely people who face their God in the stillness of nature or between the narrow walls of their often cheerless abode. As obligatory prayer in Judaism does not eliminate spontaneous praying, neither does community prayer rule out individual praying. However, Jewish tradition does attach greater importance to the praying of the community than to that of an individual soul, however ecstatic such individual prayer may be. The prayer of the community is never despised. One can pray because God is near, but God is nearer to the community than to the individual. When ten people pray, the Divine Presence is with them, for "God stands in the divine assembly" (Ps. 82:1). King David, praying by himself, had to seek an *et ratzon*, "a moment of favor" for his prayer (Ps. 69:14). But the prayer of the community is heard at all times: "'Surely this great nation

2. I use the term "prescribed" here rather than "obligatory," because while *tefillat tzibbur* is on the whole obligatory, it need not always be so. The order and the text of the service on fast days which are specially proclaimed in case of an emergency are prescribed, but the prayers as such are not *tefillat ḥova.*

is a wise and understanding people!' For what other great nation has God so close to it as the Lord our God is to us whenever we call out to Him?" (Deut. 4:6–7). If one is unable to join the community in the synagogue, one should at least pray at the same time as the community is praying (Berakhot 6a).

Rabbi Yehuda HaLevi in the *Kuzari*, explaining the importance of community prayer, says:

> Common prayer has many advantages. In the first instance, a community will never pray for a thing which is hurtful to the individual, whilst the latter sometimes prays for something to the disadvantage of other individuals… One of the conditions of prayer, craving to be heard is that its object be profitable to the world, but not hurtful in any way. Another (advantage of community prayer) is that an individual rarely accomplishes his prayer without slips and errors. It has been laid down, therefore, that the individual recites the prayers of a community… so that one make up for the forgetfulness or the error of the other. In this way, a complete prayer is gained, read with unalloyed devotion… For the Divine Influence is as the rain which waters an area – if deserving of it – and includes some smaller portion which does not deserve it but shares the general abundance. On the other hand, rain is withheld from an area which does not deserve it, although some portion is included which did deserve it but suffers with the majority… A person who prays but for himself is like him who retires alone into his house, refusing to assist his fellow citizens in the repair of their walls. His expenditure is as great as his risk. He, however, who joins the majority spends little, yet remains in safety, because one replaces the defects of the other. (*Kuzari* 3:19, Hartwig Hirschfeld translation)

This interpretation is of great interest because it throws into relief another of the problematic aspects of individual prayer. The self-centeredness of such prayer may amount to outright selfishness and may lead to unethical praying. It is not at all contrary to the dignity of God that man should pray to Him for a piece of bread, but it is unethical prayer if he prays for something that can only be had to the detriment of others.[3] Equally noteworthy is the second implication of HaLevi's interpretation. Those rare personalities who in prayer alone fly to the Alone are so much in love with their personal salvation that they may become easily forgetful of the lot of humanity that is less gifted in seeking the way to God. In community prayer, the hearts of those less able to pray as one should may be awakened and carried along on the waves of communal inspiration.

Most significant, however, is HaLevi's thought that the community is one entity and the prayers of the people that constitute it unite into one prayer. The concept derives directly from the specific nature of Judaism. Judaism is not a religion of individual souls but that of a people. This again is due to the fact that Judaism is not a creed in the sense that one should be saved by faith alone; in Judaism one must implement one's belief and one's deeds. The deed, however, is life in its entirety, and life in its entirety is never life in isolation, not even that of the individual. The whole of life, in all its manifestations, personal or political, ethical or economical, individual or social, must be lived with the awareness that it is being enacted by man in the presence of God. This is not a task for an individual, but for mankind as a whole; and until such time when mankind as a whole may embrace the responsibility, it will be realizable only by "a smaller mankind," a people that is committed to the aspiration of living its life as a people in the Sight of God.[4] One may believe in Judaism as an individual; one can live as a Jew only together with other Jews. It is in this sense that Judaism is the religion of a people. It is the way of life of a whole people; it is the way of life that has determined the essential quality of a people. In Judaism it is not only the individual that confronts God; the people as a people is committed to living in such confrontation. As it lives as a people in the presence of God so it turns to God in prayer as a people. This is specifically Jewish. *Tefillat tzibbur* is not congregational prayer; every *minyan* is an *eida*, because it signifies

3. Jewish folklore has preserved the prayer of a professional thief who, on the Day of Atonement was overheard pleading: Almighty God, should it be Your will that anyone of Your children be punished with loss by theft, may it be Your will that the punishment be executed through me.
4. See Eliezer Berkovits, *God, Man and History: A Jewish Interpretation* (New York: Jonathan David, 1959), 135–42.

the whole of Israel. Jews assembled in prayer are not a congregation but a miniature national assembly at prayer.

While individual prayer has its own depth and fervor, which is not easily paralleled by community prayer, the latter too has certain qualities which are unique to it. That an individual should recognize his dependence on God is a common occurrence. One would normally assume that to sense a transcendental presence about man and to be aware of an unceasing debt of gratitude to God are sentiments of which only the individual soul is capable, but not an entire people as such. With Israel, prayer is a national preoccupation. As the *Mekhilta* puts it, for Jews prayer is an *umanut*, a national profession, as it were (*Mekhilta* 14:10). In the armory of the Jewish people prayer is a major weapon of national survival. The unique religious quality of *tefillat tzibbur* lies in the fact that through it an entire people, independently of the dramatic impact of a momentary experience, as a matter of its daily routine declares its complete dependence on God, affirms as a people its faith in God's providence and acknowledges as a people that it could not exist for a second without the unending mercies of God. This is something unparalleled in the history of the human race; and it has a depth and a fervor which are unknown to individual prayer.

Judaism is fully aware of the religious inspiration which one may derive from confronting God in the solitude of one's most personal sorrow or joy; but Jews are able to derive no less inspiration from standing before God in the midst of the community. The intimacy of the confrontation with God may become even more real for a Jew when seeking His nearness together with other Jews. What the stillness of approaching God alone may do for other people, the waves of the praying voices of the community may do for a Jew. This is due to that specific quality of Jewish religiosity that I have discussed. The most singularly personal aspect of the piety of a Jew is significant because it remains within the context of the religious faith, the affirmations and commitments, of all Israel. A Jew, who, overwhelmed by the mystical grandeur of God's creation, falls on his knees and worships the Creator, is engaged in an act of individual piety. However, if he does so as an individual, without the realization that it is "our God and God of our fathers" whom he worships, without incorporating in his personal experience a sense of unity with the Jews of all ages who worshipped the same God before him, his individual piety is not Jewish. It is bound to have a quality which, from the religious point of view, will prove to be un-Jewish.

All individual piety among Jews is validated by the closeness of its contact with the strivings and experiences of the people of God in all ages. Individual piety in Judaism has two roots: in the soul of the individual and in the soul of all Israel. Because of that, a Jew is never by himself in prayer. At the most lonely moments of his life, if he prays as a Jew, he prays with other Jews, with all the Jews who ever prayed before him and with all those who still pray. In a very palpable sense, Jewish praying is one. Every individual Jew, even if he is all by himself with his Maker, prays with all other Jews; every community of praying Jews is united in prayer with all other communities; and all communities of any single generation are linked by Jewish prayer to all the communities of all generations that ever approached God in prayer. It is for this reason that communal prayer may bring to a Jew an original freshness of experience and depth of devotion which purely personal praying may never grant him. *Tefillat tzibbur* is really one prayer; it is the prayer of one people; it is the individual prayer of a people.

The idea has found its formulation in a number of halakhic rules, which regulate the direction in which Jews should face when praying. Those Jews who live in the Diaspora should face in prayer in the direction of the Holy Land. Those in Eretz Yisrael should turn toward Jerusalem. In Jerusalem, one should face toward the place of the Holy Temple… therefore, those who stand in the east face west; in the west, they turn east. From the north, one faces southward; from the south, northward. "As a result, all Israel directs its heart toward their Father in Heaven."[5] In Jewish prayer, as the individual confronts God, he is at the

5. The version in the Talmud in Berakhot 30a states that "all Israel directs its heart toward one place." Our quotation is from *Tur* (*Ohr HaḤayim*, no. 94). Either the author had a somewhat different version before him or he interpreted the talmudic text in this manner. There is no doubt that "one place" in the Talmud does not refer to a point in space but to "their Father in Heaven." One may see it clearly by the beginning of the *baraita*, amid a discussion about a blind person praying in synagogue. Facing toward the sanctuary has clearly the symbolical meaning of directing the attention of the heart toward God.

same time part of a praying nation. All Israel, united in devotion, stands before God in prayer.

There is a midrash which gives poetic expression to the thought in the following words: "Rabbi Pinḥas said it in the name of Rabbi Meir and Rabbi Yirmeya, in the name of Rabbi Ḥiya bar Abba: When Israel prays, you do not find that they all pray together. Every synagogue prays by itself. Now, after all the synagogues have completed praying, the angel who is in charge of prayer takes all the prayers which were recited in all the synagogues and makes them into a crown and places them on the head of the Lord ... thus we read also in the book of Isaiah: 'Israel, through you I am glorious' (Is. 49:3), meaning that the Lord wears the prayers of Israel like a crown, as it were" (Exodus Rabba 21:4). The prayers of all Israel are presented to God as one. Innumerable individual prayers are offered to God by individuals and by congregations of individuals; only the *Am Eḥad* prays as one people. An entire people as a people, not only as a congregation of individuals; as part of the normal routine of its daily existence, and not only on specific occasions; as a form of its basic means of survival, and not only as a compliment to the Almighty – an entire people bows down and worships and thanks. It is prayer unsurpassed in the history of the human race. It is the crown of all praying.

What Is *Kavana*?

We have discussed the various problematic aspects of spontaneous, individual prayer. For the sake of greater clarity, I shall list them here together and indicate once again concisely how the problems are met. At the beginning of all outpouring of the heart, we encountered the dilemma of confrontation with God whose presence one assumes to plead with Him about His absence. Individual prayer, elicited by specific occasions, may imply that man seeks, praises, and thanks God only occasionally, whereas man's dependence and God's nearness are perennial. Every occasion is an occasion for prayer. Finally, we found that individual prayer may be selfish and unethical prayer, completely forgetful of the interests of one's fellow men. We may, therefore, say that individual prayer is problematic because of the insufficiency of the subjective experience of the individual alone; because it takes insufficient cognizance of the objectively ever acute human dependence on God; and because it tends to overlook the intricate web of interdependence between all human destinies. The problems arise as regards the individual, as regards God, as regards society.

We have seen how these difficulties were met by letting all individual praying be supported by its contact with the religious experience of all Israel, by complementing the free prayer by obligatory services, and by putting emphasis on the importance of community prayer. We have also seen that Judaism could proceed in the manner indicated because both obligatory and communal prayer were not artificial creations, conceived specifically for the purpose of solving problems, but that they represent a facet of the specific nature of Jewish religiosity. Since Judaism is the religion of a people, and not that of believing individuals, it is natural for Jews to pray even individually in the context of the objective religious experience of all Israel and as part of the praying people.

The question may, however, no longer be put off; does not free personal prayer have a depth of emotion and intensity which by its very nature obligatory and prescribed communal prayer may never achieve? The very absence of the specific occasion may blight the force of the sentiment. The continuous repetition of the same prayers may reduce the text to mere litany, and praying to a purely mechanical activity without much spiritual significance. This, of course, is possible. Obligatory communal prayer has its problems no less than individual prayer. However, the dividing line between right and wrong praying is not identical with the distinction between free and obligatory prayer. From time immemorial, the teachers of Judaism have been aware of the dangers of reducing prayer to a mere litany. The Talmud records the saying of Rabbi Eliezer: "He who makes his prayer a fixed routine, his prayer is not an appeal for God's grace" (Berakhot 28b). The implication is that such activity is not prayer. Rabbi Shimon pointed to the very essence of prayer; when expressing the same thought more elaborately, he said: "Do not make your prayer something automatic, but a plea for compassion before God, for it is said: "for he is gracious and compassionate, slow to anger, abounding in kindness, and renouncing punishment" (Avot 2:13). Rabbi Shimon draws our attention to the utter futility of prayer as mere litany and routine. Now, if God were the stern ruler and master, and prayer, a verbal tribute to Him, then mechanical recitation might make sense. Since, however, prayer is only possible because God is gracious and merciful and in His loving-kindness considers man, the approach to Him can only be one of longing for His love and mercy.

What Rabbi Shimon really implies is that even in obligatory prayer, the confrontation with the Divine Presence should be undertaken with the same immediacy of approach as in personal prayer. Even though the prayer is prescribed, one should not offer it as if one were performing a "burdensome" duty (Berakhot 29b). As in free individual prayer, so also in regulated communal worship one should seek the Divine Presence in an act of personal confrontation. The prayer is prescribed, yet one should recite it as a personal offering, as if it were the free outpouring of one's own heart.

The question, of course, is: Is this possible? Can it be done? No doubt, it is far from being an easy task; but it has often been accomplished, and even only partial success along this line of religious endeavor is no mean achievement. The way by which it is to be accomplished is indicated by the term *kavana*. The word does not mean so much concentration on the text, but rather – with the help of concentrating on the meaning of the text – to achieve a directedness of being toward the one who confronts man, i.e., God. So it is taught, "He who prays should direct his heart toward Heaven" (Berakhot 31a). Maimonides defines *kavana* in the following words: "What is *kavana*? One should remove from one's heart all other thoughts and see oneself as if one were standing before the Divine Presence" (*Mishneh Torah, Hilkhot Tefilla* 4:16). One should evacuate one's heart in order that it may be filled completely with the consciousness of standing in the presence of God. This is, of course, the original situation of free personal prayer at its finest. By means of *kavana,* a Jew transforms the obligatory prayer into the voice of his own heart. As the result of *kavana,* the prayer of Israel becomes one's very own in a most personal sense. This restoration of the original prayer situation in obligatory prayer is so important that, on the basis of the Talmud, Maimonides formulates the principle that "any prayer that is recited without *kavana* is no prayer" (*Mishneh Torah, Hilkhot Tefilla* 4:15).

Every possible effort is to be made to induce *kavana*. The place of prayer, the structure of the building, the ground on which one stands, should be chosen with the view in mind of facilitating *kavana* (Berakhot 34b); as Rashi put it: "that man may direct his heart heavenward and his heart may become contrite." In order to counter the danger of prayer becoming a matter of routine, one is required to prepare oneself for prayer, dwelling for a few moments in restful meditation prior to praying; and at the conclusion of the service one tarries as if unwilling to depart (Berakhot 29b). Of the *Ḥasidim HaRishonim* it is reported that they would sit in long wordless meditation before prayer and after it, each phase of meditation being equal in duration to the time spent in praying. While free individual prayer is spontaneous, through *kavana* one strives to establish the intimacy and ever-renewed freshness of the confrontation with God. While individual prayer receives its fervor from the impact of the specific occasion which elicits it, *kavana* transforms prayer itself into a specific occasion. Through *kavana,* every obligatory service becomes indeed a service of the heart, an occasion for the heart. Because of *kavana,* every obligatory prayer, notwithstanding the sameness of the text and the regularly recurring occasion, may become a unique religious experience which is unrepeatable.

The place of *kavana* in Jewish prayer is of such importance that, originally, it was taught that a person who is unable to concentrate should not pray. The father of the great Babylonian Amora, Shmuel, would not pray for three days after a long exhausting journey, until he could recover his strength and mental alertness (Eiruvin 65a). From the point of view of ideal prayer, any kind of preoccupation or concern and worry which does not allow a person to concentrate on the act of praying exempts a Jew from the obligation to pray.[1] On the basis of talmudical teachings, Maimonides lays down the rule: "Finding that one's mind is confused and the heart preoccupied, one must not pray until one has regained calmness and composure" (*Mishneh Torah, Hilkhot Tefilla* 4:15). If the idea is followed to its final consequences, it would seem to imply that a specific situation of crisis is the least conducive to obligatory communal prayer. In such a situation, man's preoccupation with the moment robs him of the ability to render the prescribed service with *kavana.* Rather interestingly, Rabbeinu Tam (Eiruvin 65a), explaining a difficulty arising from a talmudic text, says: "When in trouble, do not pray."

As we saw earlier in our discussion, too intense a preoccupation with one's own troubles may be a barrier to the approach to God. He who is too much concerned with his woes confronts mainly himself and does not stand with full awareness in the presence of God. In the case of individual prayer, we found the solution in the not-too-easy task of turning to God with such childlike trust as to make Him the confidant

1. It should, however, be remembered that in our times the absence of *kavana* does not require a repetition of the prayer. For the reasons, see *Tur, Ohr HaḤayim* 78:20.

of one's sorrow. However, self-centered intensity of the specific experience may so absorb human attention as to render obligatory prayer impossible. A person may be so preoccupied with the specific moment as to be incapable of performing the act of *kavana,* which alone may breathe life into prescribed prayer. A man preoccupied with the moment may not be able to embrace in sincerity the basic principle of obligatory prayer, that is, that at all moments man is equally dependent on God and that at all times God is indeed near. Without *kavana,* however, prayer is mere verbiage.

We see now how the problems inherent in free individual prayer have swung the wheel of our thought around in a complete circle. Prayer originates as the spontaneous outpouring of the heart in response to the crisis of a distinct situation. The mature religious understanding that the human situation as such asks for continuous prayer leads to obligatory communal prayer. However, this kind of prayer, in order to preserve the sense of personal confrontation with God, which is essential, requires *kavana.* The ever-renewed effort of directing the heart's attention toward God alone makes prayer a unique response to the true religious quality of the undramatic normalcy of man's daily routine. It may now happen that a specific crisis situation, which serves as the original release for a praying response, may blot out the realization that all moments are alike, moments of creaturely need of God. Thus the specific moment, which may lead to individual prayer, may make man unfit for obligatory prayer at the moment.

What are the resources which will enable a Jew to pray with *kavana* and thus transform prescribed communal prayer into the personal voice of the individual? We believe that they are manifold. The principles which are incorporated in prescribed prayer are indeed of a general nature, but in the sense that they apply to every individual. These principles of God's eternal presence, of man's perennial dependence, and of unceasing divine providence, interpreting the human situation, do indeed interpret the situation of every human being. However unique the personal situation of a man may be, it is only a variant of the general situation of man, and this not in theory but in actual living reality. In all its uniqueness, every individual human condition means living before God, being dependent on Him and sustained by Him. For this reason, a Jew is able to understand his individual life experience in terms of the ideas and sentiments that inform the prescribed order of service in Judaism. Far from allowing a gap to remain between the individual experience and the general aspirations of Jewish prayer, through *kavana* the general concepts become the crystallization of the meaning of the individual experience. Through *kavana*, the relationship between God and man – as conceived by prescribed prayer – becomes a reality. The idea becomes an actual experience, but only because when praying, one sees one's own life interpreted and illuminated. The general affirmations of obligatory and communal prayer may indeed be made to speak with the warmth and intimacy of personal prayer, because they do reflect the human situation as looked upon from the angle of every individual human circumstance.

Furthermore, the general concepts which direct Jewish prayer are – as we have learned already – not general in the sense of being the outcome of a philosophical or theological theory, but rather in the sense that they represent the corporate historic experience of the Jewish people. It is against the background of this experience that we praise, affirm in faith, and thank. But the corporate experience of all Israel has always exercised a determining influence on the personal destiny of the individual Jew. In fact, one might say that the Jewish quality of all individual destiny among Jews derives from its connection with the corporate destiny of all Israel. It is because of this that the Jew, invoking God in the incorporated prayers of His people and relating his individual destiny to that of the people, may feel that the words and the thoughts are his very own, most befitting his own personal condition. All this is again strengthened by the fact that Judaism, as we have already had occasion to point out, is the religion of a people. All individual piety is significantly Jewish only insofar as it is a manifestation in a unique situation of the faith and commitment, of the way of life, of Israel. Because of this, the most spontaneous and free personal prayer of a Jew is only a facet of the corporate prayer of the Jewish people. As I have maintained in a previous chapter, even when he prays all by himself, a Jew is in the company of a praying Israel. Thus, the need for individual prayer may find satisfaction in the obligatory prayer of the synagogue. As obligatory prayer in Judaism is the individual prayer of the people, so may – by means of *kavana* – the prayer of the people become the personal prayer of the individual.

As a Jew praises God as the Shield of Abraham, through historic and spiritual identification he praises Him also as his own personal Helper and Protector. When he supplicates, "Heal us, Lord, and we shall be healed, save us and we shall be saved," the individual Jew may be in perfect health and enjoying all reasonable security, and yet he may pray so from his own personal situation, acknowledging that he is in good health because, indeed, God is an ever-present Healer, and that he is safe and comfortable because God is his Savior. He does not pray in the singular, but in the plural; he does not pray only for himself, but associates himself with others, who pray like him or do not pray at all. The others will be first of all those closest to him, his immediate family, his friends, his people; but the term may include anyone by means of *kavana*. It is our *kavana* that brings the words to life and allows us to take possession of the text, as it were, for the purpose of our own praying. When we conclude the entreaty with the words "Blessed are You, Lord, who heals His people Israel," the supplication does not become impersonal by reference to the people. On the contrary, the Jew may turn to the Healer, praying for himself and for all those whom he cares to include in his prayer, because God is the healer of all. His personal faith in God, the Healer, is supported by the corporate experience of Israel who has known Him through the ages as its healer.

The Jew knows God as the healer of all and in a most personal sense as his very own healer, because He has made Himself known to Israel as the healing God. Nor is it different in the case of thanksgiving. We thank God three times daily for His miracles and beneficence "that are daily with us," because they are indeed always with us. The plural, us, includes first of all oneself. What we are saying means, of course, "that are daily with me." It is a personal prayer in the true sense of the word. In the midst of the dull routine of an utterly unexciting individual life it may of course be rather difficult to appreciate the need for thanksgiving as a personal one. In such a situation, the plural form of the thanksgiving prayer, far from weakening its meaningfulness for the individual, may even help to provide it. The emphasis that all life is sustained by the mercies of God may help me to realize that indeed His mercies are with me always. That this is so is an affirmation of faith. A Jew may make such affirmation of his own personal faith because he can address God as: "You are the Rock of our lives, the Shield of our salvation through every generation." For the Jew, "the Rock of our lives" is the Rock of his own personal life in the most intimate sense, and even more so because He is "the Rock of our lives."

There is one more means by which the prescribed community prayer may be rendered meaningful in relationship to the individual. It can be done by linking to the normal situation, to which obligatory prayer refers, any specific situation or occasion of a person, and by incorporating free individual prayer, fitting for the specific condition, in the prescribed text for all conditions. As has been pointed out earlier, the introduction of obligatory prayer did not eliminate the original spontaneous and purely personal prayer.

Since, however, the two exist side by side, it was quite natural that the question of their relationship to each other should have arisen. When a man, in a moment of personal trouble, is impelled to implore God in individual prayer, but it is also a time appointed for obligatory prayer, what should he do first? Does the obligatory prayer come first or the private one? While some give preference to private prayer and others to the obligatory one, the decision is in accordance with a third opinion, which requires that one should include private supplication in the paragraph of *Shome'a Tefilla*, "Hearer of Prayer." One may also include private supplication in each of the appropriate general supplications of the *Shemoneh Esreh*. Thus, Rabbi Ḥiya bar Ashi says in the name of Rav: "Even though it has been said that one should plead for one's private needs in 'Hearer of Prayer,' nevertheless, if someone is sick in one's house, one may include an individual prayer for him in 'the Blessing for the Sick'; if one is in need of livelihood, one may include one's private intercession in 'the Blessing of the Years'" (Avoda Zara 8a).

The same may be done in the case of every other specific need of a person. The general supplications of the *Amida* have been formulated with a view to the human situation. As Maimonides put it: "They represent the categories of all needs of the individual and of society" (*Mishneh Torah, Hilkhot Tefilla* 1:4). As the Jew introduces his private prayers into the prescribed text, he is free to pour out his heart in his own words and in accordance with his own personal woe and sorrow. He can do it naturally, as indicated above, because of the very close connection between the historic and religious destiny of the individual Jew and that of all Israel. However, as he does so, obligatory and free prayer coalesce into the most intimate and most fervent personal prayer of the Jew, who, although he prays only for himself, and only now, prays all the more significantly since he does not pray by himself.

There is one more question that I wish to consider in connection with the theme of this chapter. For many centuries now, the obligatory prayers of Judaism have been given definite form and contents. The text has been established, the order of the services set. Traditionally, Jews pray today as they prayed a thousand and more years ago. Is it conceivable that, from a literary point of view, a text should retain its meaningfulness with respect to each contemporary human situation for such a long period of time? Is it not to be expected that both the intellectual and emotional contents should become outdated and empty for a new generation?

Furthermore, will not the continuous repetition of the same text become monotonous and stifle the thoughts and emotions of the person who tries to express himself through them in prayer? It would be futile to discuss these and related questions purely academically. Only the facts can provide the answer. It is a fact that numerous Jews do feel that the established prayers of Judaism have become outdated for them. It is also a fact that numerous Jews do daily identify themselves with these prayers with the same ease and naturalness as Jews were able to do the first time these prayers were formulated. It would indeed be inane to assume that the latter represent the obscurantist, medieval type, whereas those of the first group are the modern enlightened Jews.

There are today tens of thousands of Jews the world over, as there were in all ages, who are in no way intellectually inferior to their brethren in the liberal or Reform groups and who have no less keen a grasp of the ideas and values of contemporary culture and civilization than they, who nevertheless are able to pray significantly within the ages-old order of service, reciting the words of the text as if they were the creations of their own hearts. It is equally a fact that to this day, the religious services of Orthodox synagogues, adhering to the old patterns and to the old texts, are unequaled in religious intensity and fervor, as well as immediacy of experience, by the services of modern temples which have been devised and formulated in conformity with modern concepts and present-day religious sensitivity. For those who accept them, the old order and the old texts are alive and more up-to-date than the modern texts and services are for their own protagonists. The reason for the inability of so many Jews to identify themselves with the traditional prayers of Israel in our days may be explained by a measure of personal Jewish-religious inadequacy no less satisfactorily than by reference to a possible inadequacy of the prayers and services themselves.

It is, however, not my intention here to criticize Jews but to attempt to explain Jewish prayer. I shall, therefore, limit myself to trying to indicate those literary qualities of Jewish prayer which render them ageless for so many contemporary Jews. I make mention here of the literary qualities alone because as to contents and basic ideas it may be enough to refer to what has been said in the immediately preceding section of this chapter on the resources of *kavana*. The classical Jewish prayer of the *Amida*, in its manifold variations for all the occasions on which it is recited, has a poetic dignity which is cast in the mold of – seemingly – artless simplicity. The text is a treasure house of biblical allusions. Every phrase and every thought has its biblical parallel and has been formulated in the image of a biblical text. Yet, the *Amida* shows the beauty and the depth of a great and original literary creation. As literature, it is only second to the Bible. It has a quality of literary timelessness akin to that of the Bible. Like the Bible, it combines simplicity with depth. As the Bible may be read and studied by children, adults, and the aged, so may the *Amida* be prayed by all age groups of Jews, and each one may find significance in it, commensurate with one's own depth and situation. As the Bible may speak to all men at all times in all situations, just because it surpasses the limitations of the personal and timely, in a similar way the classical Jewish prayer has succeeded in expressing what is lastingly present in all individual Jewish prayer beyond all limitations of the now and the here. Because of that quality, every Jew in each generation may be led to his own personal confrontation with God by way of the prayer of all Israel.

As the Bible itself, so has the *Amida* too been interpreted through the ages; yet to this day, as with the Bible, new treasures of thought and sentiments may be revealed in it to the one who has his roots deep in timeless Judaism and who, at the same time, is seriously engaged in man's contemporary search for a personally meaningful human destiny. Paraphrasing a talmudic saying about the Bible, it may be said in a related sense of classical Jewish prayer: every time you recite it, it should be as if you would recite it for the first time. It should be, because it can be. It is all up to you. The "Men of the Great Assembly" who, according to tradition, composed the *Amida*, did not imprint their own timebound condition on their creation. In the timeless mold of prophetic tradition and inspiration, they have taught all Israel to pray to God, each one in his time and in his condition. However, what has been said about the *Amida*, which is the prayer par excellence in Judaism, applies – though to a lesser degree – to the other prayers which constitute the order of the obligatory communal service.

It is interesting to note that while from the halakhic point of view one may pray in any language which one understands (Sota 32a) – and indeed a number of prayers in Aramaic were in time added to the original service because it was a language spoken by Jews – Jewries who oriented their life according to the halakha have nevertheless refused to depart from the original Hebrew of the prayers. No doubt, this is partly due to the realization that Jews pray as one people. A translation of the community service into the vernacular spoken by each Jewry would have undermined the sense of unity with which Jews stand in prayer as a people before God. However, perhaps of even greater importance has been this stubborn adherence to the original language because of the unique quality of the text itself. All translation is interpretation, and all interpretation is time bound and situation-conditioned. All translations of the *Amida* shatter the quality of timelessness which is inseparable from the original. At best, a translation may become a not very original individual prayer of the translator, or a congregational prayer of a small group which shares the translator's idea, literary taste, and religious attitude. At worst, it might be a fine – or not so fine – literary exercise. There has been only one way of retaining the ageless quality of the classical Jewish prayer, that is, not to pray it in translation.

Influencing God?

Independently of the importance that the mere fact of the confrontation with God in prayer may have for the life of man, prayers of supplication desire that God may intervene in the normal course of events for the sake of the supplicant. The idea, which is implied in this kind of praying, has come under severe criticism almost since the day that man has ever started to pray. The questioning may be undertaken on philosophical and theological grounds, but it may also be the result of a sensitive religious conscience. Speaking philosophically or theologically, it has been doubted that God could be expected to change His plans with the world to fulfill man's personal wishes. From the religious point of view, it has been occasionally asserted that a man trusting in God should not attempt to change the will of God for him in any situation.

At first I shall take a closer look at the philosophical objections. The nature of some of these objections is well illustrated by the way a man like Voltaire would pray. He would say: "O God of all worlds and of all beings, the only prayer which is befitting to You is submission, for why pray to Him who has ordered all things, foreseen all things, and linked together all things in a chain from the very beginning?"[1] This was quite logical for Voltaire. According to his deistic philosophy, God

1. Heiler, *Prayer*, 92.

created the world, established its laws in the light of universal reason, and cut the umbilical cord – as it were – completely between Himself and His creation. The divinity as such is completely removed from its creation, which functions independently by the force of its inherent lawfulness, which was preordained by the creator. Within such a system, nothing can happen except in conformity with, and as a result of, the laws of the cosmos itself.

All supplication is futile in such a situation. This indeed follows from a deistic philosophy. If the creator, having done his job, has left the world to its own devices, letting it function by way of universal laws implanted within it, then of course he is unapproachable by man as he himself does not approach man. Prayer is meaningful only on the basis of a theistic worldview. One may pray only because one is able to believe that even after the act of creation, God has remained with the world, that indeed He renews daily the works of creation. One is able to believe this only within the context of revelational religion. We know of His presence, because He has made His presence known; we know that He is near, because He has indeed been near. We may turn to Him in prayer, because He has turned to man in revelation. The deistic argument against prayer is really directed not against prayer as such, but against revelational religion. But because of that, it need not detain us here. It is indeed so that prayer is meaningful only within a theistic universe.

Actually, it is the deistic prayer of a Voltaire which is meaningless, because it makes no sense on the basis of his own premises. If "God has departed the earth" and man cannot stand before Him, he cannot offer Him even Voltaire's prayer of submission. Moreover, if all things have been "ordered, foreseen and linked together in a chain from the beginning," if one is part of a cosmos which is ruled by impersonal and unbreakable universal laws, even submission has little moral or spiritual value. Only where there is freedom to rebel is submission a decision and a deed. To submit in a deterministic universe is simply not being a fool. If one pursued the thought to its ultimate consequences, one would have to say that in such a universe there is indeed nothing else left for a man to do but to submit, and this not only when he feels inclined to pray but also when it comes to human activity of any kind. Ethical activity, for instance, requires an area of freedom, where man may choose and decide with personal responsibility. Ethical action is only possible in a world in which all things are not ordered and linked together in a chain from the beginning. But if such freedom is assumed for ethics, why should it be impossible to assume its reality for prayer as well?

More to the point has been Kant's criticism of prayer.[2] He has expressed the opinion that in prayer man attempts to deflect God from the plan of His wisdom for the sake of some momentary benefit for himself. How could man hope that God might change His plans, conceived in His Omniscience, and be guided by the wishes of a mere man? Kant called the attempt an unseemly and impudent delusion, a molesting of God with one's importunings. No doubt, Kant's criticism does sound logical. But once again, one cannot help perceiving how easily the same kind of criticism may be directed against every form of ethical obligation. What does it really matter whether so insignificant a creature as man adheres to the categorical imperative or not? Surely, the plans of God's wisdom could not be affected by what man may do one way or another! Kant is here applying to prayer the question of Job: "If I have sinned, what have I done to You?" (Job 7:20). It is no more logical to maintain that man's failure would make no dent in the divine scheme of things than to argue that human entreaty could make no impression on that scheme. If the divine plan for the universe allows a measure of importance to man's action, it should be conceivable that the same plan may have a provision by which human suffering may also be considered a matter of some importance.

Never have philosophy and religion spoken more at cross purposes than in the case of prayer. The talmudic and midrashic teachers of Judaism saw clearly that prayer was – in a sense – tactless, that it was a form of molesting the Almighty. Yet, they prayed importunately; but never laboring under any delusion, for they were fully conscious that in prayer they were – as one might say – imposing on God. It sounds almost as a direct rebuttal of the Kantian position, about fourteen centuries before Kant, when the Midrash remarks: "A human being may have a patron, whom he approaches for assistance. If he will trouble him

2. Immanuel Kant, *Religion within the Bounds of Bare Reason*, trans. Werner S. Pluhar (Indianapolis, IN: Hackett, 2009), 165–211.

too much, the patron will cease supporting him. The Lord is not like this. As long as one is willing to impose on Him, one will be received." The same thought is expressed in more emphatic versions, for instance when it is said: "God is not like this; but the more a person beseeches Him with his needs and requests, the more God loves him"; or again, when it is maintained: "But God is not like this! The more Israel makes a nuisance of itself by thronging God's house of prayer, the greater the joy before Him" (*Midrash Tehillim* 4:3).

The teachers of Judaism were aware, no less than Kant himself, that prayer was like an imposition on God; but obviously they had a different understanding of the meaning of prayer than Kant had. According to them, prayer is possible only because God desires to be imposed upon by man. We shall see presently how this is to be understood. However, let us also note first that the masters of Jewish prayer visualized no less clearly than Kant the insignificance of the content matter of our supplications in relationship to the wisdom of the Almighty. However, far from seeing in it a hindrance to prayer, they conceived it as its very foundation. They never ceased impressing on the Jew that it is with his insignificance alone that he may approach God. For instance, when they declare: "the creature can have no claim on its creator" (Deuteronomy Rabba 2:1), they say in their own style what may be expressed philosophically by saying that the disproportion between human aspirations and the plans of divine wisdom is unbridgeable. I had occasion to quote in a previous chapter the principle of Jewish prayer: *Ein gavhut lifnei Hashem*, that man cannot stand before God with any sense of self-importance. According to halakhic rule, a Jew reciting the *Amida* has to bow down several times. However, if he is the high priest, he has to bow at the beginning and at the end of each blessing. But the king bowed his head at the beginning of the prayer and did not raise it until he finished praying. As Rashi explains it: "The higher a man's position, the more humble he must stand before God" (Berakhot 34b).

Nothing could be further from the truth than to imagine that prayer requires self-humiliation. What we have before us is the only solution to the philosophical problem of prayer. In the sight of the plans of God, conceived in omniscience and executed with omnipotence, no man's wish or desire may claim any attention because of his importance.

He may hope to be heard only in the name of his infinite insufficiency, standing in creaturely nakedness before the Infinitely Perfect. Man can do that, not because of what he is but only because of what God is.

Philosophy and religion are talking at cross purposes about prayer because they have divergent concepts about God. From the philosophical point of view, God is the Absolute, the Infinite; He is omnipotent and omniscient. This is what, in midrashic terminology, we indicate by the simple Hebrew word *raḥok,* that is, far-removed. One might say that the basic religious statement about God is that in spite of all philosophical reasoning, the *Raḥok* is, as a matter of fact, also the *Karov,* the Near One. With this affirmation stands or falls all revelational religion. It is the rock on which Judaism has been established and has survived. The idea has been expressed, for instance, by Rabbi Pinḥas in the name of Rabbi Yehuda. Other teachers have illustrated it by drawing attention to one of the noblest passages in the book of Isaiah, where we read:

> Thus says the high, the exalted One,
> abiding forever, whose name is holy:
> High and holy I abide –
> yet I am with the crushed and humbled,
> giving life to the humbled,
> giving life to crushed men's hearts. (Is. 57:15)

Realizing the full weight of these words, they observed: "Even though He is the High and Lofty One, He dwells with the one of a contrite and humble spirit" (*Midrash Tehillim* 4:3). Philosophy knows God as the High and Lofty One; in religion He is the High and Lofty One who dwells with the lowly. One cannot pray to the High and Lofty One; one cannot help praying to the High and Lofty One who, breaking through the barriers of His Infinitude, bends down to keep company with the lowly and the humble. Indeed, one may pray only because God wishes to be imposed upon. Notwithstanding His omnipotence, He considers our weakness; in spite of His omniscience, He does not despise our foolishness. Notwithstanding? In spite of? One ought to say, perhaps, more truly: such is His omniscience and omnipotence that they are one with His infinite mercy. Man may pray, because God invites him to bring his burden unto Him that He may carry it along with him (Rosh HaShana 26b). That is the kind of God He is; that is why He is God.

Kant's God is great, but not great enough; therefore, one cannot pray to him. The One who is omniscient and omnipotent in such a manner that He can even bend down and lend an ear to the supplication of a poor fool is greater. He alone is God. Is this a small matter in comparison with the universal plans of divine wisdom? The brilliance of the milky way may arouse us to admire the Creator; the power and wisdom that sustain the galaxies of immeasurable space may fill our hearts with awe and adoration. At every step, the magnificence of His works may be revealed to us in the smallest as well as the greatest of His creations. Unsurpassed in grandeur and majesty, however, is the fact that the One who wields all that power and wisdom is also the One who seeks out the company of man. That prayer is possible, that man can approach God because God desires to be approached by man, is the glory of all divine glories. When the psalmist, looking up to the skies, praised God in the words "The heavens tell of God's glory; the skies proclaim His handiwork" (Ps. 19:2), he took cognizance of the plans of divine omnipotence and omniscience. Yet, he was able to conclude the psalm so begun with the prayer, so often recited by Jews, "May the words of my mouth and my heart's reflections please You, Lord, my Rock and redeemer" (Ps. 19:15). He could do so, because he knew that those very plans of omnipotence and omniscience were only part of God's more universal plan of infinite mercy. It is within that plan that prayer has its due place.

Closely related to the philosophical are the theological difficulties. One of the major problems of prayer has been defined by Rabbi Yosef Albo, in his *Sefer HaIkkarim*, in the following words: "Either God has determined that a given person shall receive a given benefit, or He has not so determined. If He has determined, there is no need of prayer; and if He has not so determined, how can prayer avail to change God's will so that He should now determine to benefit the person, when He had not so determined before?"[3]

In his solution of the problem, Albo makes a valuable contribution to the understanding of our subject. Prayer, as he rightly points out, is not a mere recitation of words. Praying is a deed. The words, in right prayer, are an event. They reflect a process of transformation that is taking place within man. The man who turns to God in prayer in sincerity is, as the result of this act, not the same man that he was before he prayed. Praying, he has changed. The effect of prayer is similar to that of *teshuva*. A divine decree may hang over a man, but it is conditional. If he returns to God, the decree may be annulled. This, however, does not really mean that the decree has been changed. It is man who has changed. It is as if he had become another person to whom the decree never applied. Similarly in the case of prayer. When prayer is fulfilled, it is not that man has succeeded in ingratiating himself with God, who grants him now what He was not willing to grant before. In the course of prayer, man has become a person to whom a different designation is due. The new decree is the outcome of the transformation of the human being, brought about by the deed of praying.

With the help of the same argument, Albo ingeniously leads us out of another theological quandary. The question has often been asked by those who thought and wrote about prayer, God being unchangeable, how can we imagine a change in the divine will as a result of prayer? Following in the footsteps of his teacher, Rabbi Hasdai Crescas, Albo answers: "As for the objection that the divine will cannot be changed by prayer, the answer is that it is the divine will in the first place that the decree should be realized if the person in question continues in the same state, and that the decree should be changed if the person's state changes."[4]

Albo's thought is deeply imbedded in Jewish tradition. Explaining the words of the psalmist, "Hearer of prayer, to You all flesh will come," the Midrash elaborates: "It is not written 'all men,' but 'all flesh.' Hence it was said: Prayer is only heard if a person makes his heart soft like

3. Yosef Albo, *Sefer HaIkkarim*, vol. 4, part 1, ed. Isaac Husik (Philadelphia: Jewish Publication Society, 1930), 160.
4. Ibid.

flesh…through return to God" (*Midrash Tehillim* 65:2). The change of the hardened heart is the essence of right praying. In another context it was taught: "The Lord does not require of the wicked either sacrifices or burnt-offerings. He desires of them *tefillat yesharim*, the prayer of the upright." In association with another text from the Psalms, the same idea is presented to us with a rare sense of religious humor. It is maintained that King David wished to be judged by God alone; for whereas his human judges would not accept a bribe, he could bribe God. And how do we know that the Lord may be bribed? It is so stated in the Bible: *Shoḥad meḥek rasha yikkaḥ*, which in a delightfully midrashic distortion of the plain sense is made to yield: "Bribes are taken from the lap of a wicked man" (Prov. 17:23). And what is the bribe that God accepts from the wicked? It is return, prayer, and deeds of charity. God addresses Himself to man saying: "My children, return to Me as long as the gates of prayer are open, for I may be bribed in this world" (*Midrash Tehillim* 17:3).

These, and related thoughts, are most strikingly focused in depth by a statement in the *Sifrei*. It is done by an interpretive elaboration on the words of the prophet Joel: "And all those who call on the name of the Lord will escape, for there will be a remnant on Mount Zion and in Jerusalem as the Lord has said; even among the survivors called by the Lord there will be a remnant" (Joel 3:5). Because of the importance of the passage, I shall quote it in full: "Is it possible for a human being to be called by the name of God? Meant is, therefore: God is called gracious, as it is written, 'The Lord is gracious and full of compassion,' so you, too, act graciously and with compassion toward others. God is called righteous, as it is written, 'For the Lord is righteous, He loves righteousness,' so you be righteous. God is called merciful, as it is written, 'For I am merciful, says the Lord,' so you be merciful. Because of this the prophet says, 'Whosoever shall call the name of the Lord shall be delivered'" (*Yalkut Shimoni* 537:1).

The idea expressed in these words is, of course, the familiar concept of the *imitatio dei*, man's responsibility of imitating God in behavior and action. Surprising, however, is the apparent departure from the masoretic punctuation of the word which seems to be the basis of the comment. The masoretic reading of the key word in question is *yikra*, which is in the active; the Midrash reads it in the passive as, *yikareh*.

Instead of "whosoever shall call on the name of the Lord" we get "whosoever shall be called by the name of the Lord." In my rendering of the *Sifrei* in English, I have retained the masoretic version of the active form, because I believe that the point the *Sifrei* wishes to make is completely missed if we assume that it is based on another reading of the text. In my opinion, it is not merely the concept of the *imitatio dei* which is enjoined on us here.

The fuller significance of the passage lies in its originality of connecting *imitatio dei* with prayer. When we call God in prayer, we are able to approach Him only because of the attributes which He activates in His dealings with His creation. We may pray to Him only because He is called *Raḥum veḤanun*, gracious and compassionate, and *Tzaddik veḤasid*, righteous and abounding in loving-kindness. But how dare one plead with God without embracing, in the moment of prayer, as guides for one's own life, those attributes of God without which prayer would not be possible? Appealing to God's mercy and loving-kindness, we ourselves must believe in mercy and loving-kindness, otherwise, there is no ground left for us on which to stand in order to confront God. One can only pray to God if one is willing to follow in one's own life the example of the divine attributes of mercy, which alone make prayer possible. The *Sifrei* draws our attention to this inherent logic of all prayer by pretending to read *yikareh* instead of *yikra*. In prayer, the two indeed become identical. Only he may call the name of God who himself is striving to be called by the attributes of God.

Another feature of the confrontation between God and man appears now in clearer relief. In our analysis thus far, I have shown that man may only pray by relying on his creaturely needfulness in the presence of God. He comes before God, making Him the confidant of his plight. He can do that because God, who inhabits eternity and dwells in "the high and holy place," keeps company with the one "who is of a contrite and humble spirit." Now, however, we realize that as man approaches God in the lowliness of his creaturely estate, he is called upon – in the very act of prayer – to imitate God. Turning to God in existential insufficiency, man is called to dignity. It is of the very majesty of God that He who dwells on high yet takes cognizance of the lowly; it is of the very core of man's dignity that he who is so lowly may yet aspire to imitate the High and Lofty One. Prayer is possible because of what God is and of what man may become. In prayer, man calls God. As man turns to God in prayer, God too calls; He calls man so to pray as to be worthy to be called by His name. Is this, perhaps, the prayer of God of which the teachers of the Talmud and the Midrash speak? It is Rabbi Yoḥanan, who in the name of Rabbi Yossi, maintains that God too prays. God's own prayer is quoted in the Talmud as follows:

> May it be acceptable before Me that My mercy conquer My anger, that My mercy overrule My other attributes, that I may conduct Myself toward My children with the attribute of mercy and deal with them not in accordance with the strictness of the law. (Berakhot 7a)

Notwithstanding the obscurity of the passage, it clearly expresses the thought that the activation of God's mercy is not a matter of divine wantonness. It does not depend altogether on the divine will, as it were. There is another factor which must be present for it to function. God Himself, as it were, depends on that factor and prays that it may be present.

What that other factor is, and to whom God's prayer may be addressed, one may learn from a Midrash which describes God's prayer somewhat differently. In connection with the words of the psalmist, "His tent is set in Salem, His abode in Zion" (Ps. 76:3), Rabbi Berakhia explains that what is meant is the place where God prays. Originally, His prayer used to be: "May it be that My children do My will that I may not have to destroy My house and My sanctuary." Since the destruction of the Temple, however, He prays: "May My children return to Me in repentance that I may bring nearer the restoration of My house and My sanctuary" (*Midrash Tehillim* 76:3). In reality, the confrontation in prayer is a form of cooperation between God and man. Man is in need to receive, and God desires to grant. God desires to grant because He is gracious and full of compassion. However, man may approach the Giver only by acknowledging the principle on which alone God's giving is based. If he does so, he still needs mercy; for without mercy, he would attempt to confront Omniscience and Omnipotence, to whom no man can turn. If, on the other hand, he seeks God without striving to imitate those divine attributes that alone cause God to dwell with the humble and the lowly, he frustrates the activation of mercy in relationship to himself. He blocks, as it were, a divine desire. God dwells with the lowly, if the lowly does not reject dwelling in the company of the High and Holy. Every prayer is a twofold supplication: man prays that he may be heard; God, that man may so pray that he can be answered. The inherent logic of mutuality in prayer is the ever-present divine prayer addressed to man.

From the position thus gained, we may now consider a rather intriguing religious objection to prayer. Our attention is directed to it by certain mystical interpretations of the meaning of faith in God, which are common to many religions. In Eckhart's parable, which I have quoted above, the sick man would not pray because he would not molest God with such trifles as his sickness. We see now even more clearly than in the earlier parts of our discussion how misplaced such signs of respect are. Eckhart was actually comparing God to that "patron" to whom, as the Midrash warned us, He should not be compared. One should indeed not approach a mighty benefactor with requests for trifles. The mightier the patron, the more valuable the object asked for ought to be. But the Lord is not like that. It is of the very essence of His greatness that He desires to be approached by us, ourselves mere trifles.

However, as we have heard, there are two more reasons why Eckhart's sick man would not pray. Since he is sick, it must be God's will that it be so, and he would not desire anything against the will of God. Furthermore, since he is sick, God must have allowed it to happen. But if so, it must be for his benefit, for the good Lord would do nothing to harm him. He would, therefore, not pray for health, which would be against his own interest. While putting it this way is, of course, a rather primitive formulation of the religious objection, one may observe the ramification of the thought even in some phases of Hasidic piety. In a time of crisis, as an affirmation of their faith in the will of God, some

Hasidic masters would not pray. In this their attitude, they are very close to the Muslim mystic who said: "To pray 'Ah Lord, turn from me this fate,' is verily sin against Him who gave it."[5] Not such is genuine Jewish prayer. It is firmly based on the words of the psalmist, "He fulfills the will of those who revere Him; He hears their cry and saves them" (Ps. 145:19). Those who fear God have desires and express them; and God fulfills their desire and saves them. Far from seeing anything unseemly in supplicating, "O God, turn this fate from me," it is exactly what Jewish prayer asks.

One wonders whether, for the same reason of surrender to the will of God, one should refrain from supplicating both for oneself or for others. If a fellow man is in trouble, should we refuse to pray because it must be the will of God and one should trust His goodness? Or should one adopt such an attitude only when in need of help oneself, but not in the case of others? On the basis of one's unquestioning faith in God's goodness, why the distinction?

According to midrashic and talmudic teaching, one may – as it were – attempt to force one's will on God. Moses, for instance, would come before God and pray for Israel *bizroa,* with unseemly violence (Deuteronomy Rabba 2:4). In one place in the Talmud, Moses's prayer for the Jewish people is compared to one who holds a fellow man tightly by his garments and does not let him go he until he has listened to him; so was Moses holding on to God in prayer, as if to say: I shall not let you go until you forgive them. Similarly, it is said that the prophets prayed to God as a woman demands of her husband the needs of her household (Berakhot 32a). While there are indications that such violent praying is only admissible when one prays for a community, being moved to plead before God under the impact of the misery of a multitude, in principle all prayer is the same. Prayer is an act of non-submission to fate, to a situation which, indeed, has arisen because God has, at least, tolerated it. Jewish prayer is like wrestling with God, in which God desires to be vanquished. Interpreting some biblical passages, the Talmud calls God "the One who is conquered in prayer by His creatures." It is observed:

5. Quoted from Heiler, *Prayer,* 192.

"A king of flesh and blood, if he is defeated, is angry. The Lord is not so. They defeat Him in prayer, and He rejoices" (Pesaḥim 119a).

We are reminded of the importunings of prayer for which God loves man all the more. It applies to man's own prayer no less than to intercession on behalf of the community. When God's decree of doom was made known to the people of Nineveh, they resolved, among other things, "cry out to God" (Jonah 3:8). The Talmud explains the word "mightily" as meaning "with impudence." Rabbi Shimon bar Ḥalafta remarked: "If impudence prevails over evil, how much more over the Benefactor of the world" (*Yalkut Shimoni* 550:6). How is all this to be understood? We believe that "impudence" is a sign of trust and confidence and intimacy. It is man's affirmation of the greatest of all miracles, that is, that God, in His infinite loving-kindness, is accessible to man's plea; that man in all his insignificance, and with all his trifling needs, may turn to Him and be heard. As we saw earlier in this chapter, Kant believed that all prayer was an improper imposition on God. And so it has proved itself to be. It is nevertheless possible, because such is God's mercy that He desires to be near man. To have faith in this God, to approach Him with the "impudence" of faith in His concern for the lowliest of His creatures is the divine service of the heart.

Since prayer has its place of importance within the universal plan of God's mercy, one cannot speak of the will of God independently of prayer. The will of God may indeed be that man prays. When a person is set upon by life's visitations and, in an act of faith in God's infinite love, takes his troubles to the Divine Presence, something new has entered the world; the situation of this man has been transformed. It is God's will that His will be changed. It is God's prayer that His will may be changed as the result of the transforming act of human prayer. Prayer is part of the scheme of divine providence. As God gave man life, so did He give him prayer, too, as an instrument of living. Let us, however, remember that the instrument of prayer cannot be misused. As we have found in our previous discussion, he who calls on God must strive to be called by the "name" of God. As man confronts God, pleading that this fate be turned from him, he purifies his desires in the image of the divine attributes which alone allow him to pray. This is his chance to be heard. The more he succeeds in being called by the "name" of God, the closer the cooperation between his desire to be heard and God's desire to answer. As a final insight into the nature of prayer, Judaism teaches that the *tzaddik* may nullify the decrees of the Almighty, that he may change divine justice to divine mercy, that he may decree and God will fulfill (Berakhot 19a). The man who may be called by the "name" of God is the one who may impose on Him most, and yet be loved most. He is the one by whom God most desires to be "defeated"; he is the one who enables God's anger to be turned into His mercy, as God Himself prays that it may.

Is Prayer Answered?

The question so often asked, whether prayer is answered or not, cannot be resolved on the basis of any theoretical discussion. Even if one could prove, on the basis of some conclusive theory, that prayer may be answered, it would amount to very little unless prayer were answered in actual fact. On the other hand, if it is a matter of human experience that prayers are answered, all theories to the contrary may be lightly dismissed.

This study of prayer has, of course, been written from the point of view of belief in the efficacy of prayer. It is the Jewish point of view, based on the Bible, talmudic and midrashic literature, and the experience of the Jewish people from the earliest times to this day. We know that prayers are answered because many of our prayers have been answered. There is no need here to enumerate all the prayers of the Bible which were answered beyond doubt. Similar experiences or prayers heard by God are on record in the Talmud and in the annals of Jewish history, and many may be known to individual Jews from their personal experiences. But, of course, prayers are not always answered. Some of the most moving prayers of the prophets and the psalmists are complaints about prayers not heard by God. Alas, how numerous are the fruitless prayers in which Israel poured out its heart in the course of its long, woe-steeped history! As to the individual, at times it would seem as if his prayers are hardly ever heard and accepted. The question for us, therefore, is not whether prayers are answered, but rather why is there – apparently – so little conclusive evidence that indeed they are.

Before I enter into a discussion of the question proper, it may be advisable to clarify a point on which I have touched earlier, which however now requires more definitive treatment. There is a chariness among certain people to admit the possibility of prayer being answered because of what may be called a dogmatic prejudice of determinism. Since all events in the world occur under the iron law of causality, it is maintained that any answer to prayer, which would bring about a result that otherwise might not be expected, would require a direct interference on the part of God with the laws of nature. Every prayer would be asking for a miracle. We fully appreciate that one may well be able to believe in the possibility of miracles and yet should reject the idea of a divine response to prayer which would constitute an interference with the laws of nature. What would indeed become of any orderliness in nature if, in response to the unceasing supplication of the human race, God would continually interfere with the natural course of events? The result would probably be like pushing the world back into the original *tohu vavohu*.

Judaism fully sympathizes with such a position and dismisses prayer against the laws of nature. According to mishnaic teaching: "he who cries that a past event be revoked prays in vain" (Berakhot 54a). For instance, says the Mishna, suppose a man's wife is pregnant. Should he pray "May it by Your will that my wife give birth to a son?" This would be a *tefillat shav*, a futile prayer. The discussion in the Gemara shows that, the sex of the embryo having been established by the laws of nature, to pray for a change would be praying for a miracle. Leah, the sister of Rachel, did indeed pray for such a miracle and her prayer was heard. However, that was an exceptional case. That she was heard was itself a miracle and *ein mazkirin maaseh nissim*, "one does not mention the miraculous" as one considers the normal rules of praying (Berakhot 60a). We believe that it is in keeping with authentic Jewish teaching to say that praying for a miracle is *tefillat shav*, a futile prayer. Not that God does not perform miracles, but miracles are not performed in response to prayer.

A Jew prays for the possible, not for the impossible. However, together with this, one must also bear in mind that Judaism takes its stand on a worldview which is not deterministic. A fact or an event already established in the course of the natural functionings of the laws of nature will not be changed in response to prayer, but as long as they have not been actually so established, their realization is not at all unequivocally determined by the rules of cause and effect. Does such a position exclude orderliness from nature? One might as well ask the modern physicist who has no longer any use for the law of causality, and acknowledges only statistical laws, whether his concepts do not throw nature into chaos. Needless to say, the Jewish worldview does not derive from present-day physics. There is however, one area of human endeavor that has been with us since time immemorial and which, in all ages, has been confronted with the problem of determinism no less than prayer, that is, ethics. No ethics may be meaningfully maintained in a strictly deterministic universe. Yet, the area of relative noncommitment, which must be assumed to exist within physical nature in order that ethics may be possible, does not automatically throw universal orderliness out of gear. Similarly, the assumption of such an area of noncommitment in nature, which is required in order to make God's free response to prayer possible, need not annul the normal functioning of the laws of the physical universe.

Shall we assume that while man may act freely in the context of nature, God may not do so? Of course, there is a problem to be faced here. The conflict of necessity versus freedom is the perennial quandary of all philosophical thought. The problem is, however, no more serious for prayer than for ethics and any form of responsible human existence. It must be possible to integrate a measure of human freedom with the orderliness of physical nature; otherwise, there could be no room for man on earth.

Whatever our theoretical solution to the problem of ethics may be, it will apply equally to that other ramification of the same problem, that of prayer. Man may turn to God in prayer because a sufficient degree of freedom is reserved for him to do so within the scheme of universal orderliness; God may answer man's prayer because He too wields freedom in such a way as to be consistent with the laws of order, which He laid down for the universe. It is not important that one should be able to spell out in detail how such dovetailing of necessity and freedom may be brought about. It is enough for one to be able to accept the idea. No less a critique of all traditional religion than Kant, for instance, accepted it. He found it necessary to believe in such ultimate harmony between necessity and freedom, in order to establish man's status as an ethical being. Faith in God – for Kant only a postulate of practical reason, for Judaism the foundation of all reality – does imply that the physical universe of necessity is meaningfully related to the spiritual one of freedom. Because of that, man may act in moral responsibility. Because of that, he may pray and God may answer, without having continuously to wreak havoc with His own laws in order to answer man's plea.

The relationship between Jewish prayer and the natural order is, in our opinion, rather well expressed in some simple words of the Tosefta to the Talmud tractate of Berakhot. It is said there: "There is a prayer which is indecent. How is that? A man gathers a hundred *kor* of grain into his barn. If he prays: may it be Your will that they be two hundred… or he has a hundred barrels of wine in his cellar, and he says: may it be Your will that they become two hundred… this is a futile prayer. But he should pray that God's blessing may enter into them and no decrease befall them" (Tosefta Berakhot 6:12).

The concept of *tefillat shav* here receives a clearer illumination. The Jew does not pray against reality; he prays that God's blessing may descend on it. The *berakha* for which we pray is not the suspension of the order of nature, but the activation of the dovetailing of the order of nature with that of freedom for the purpose of God's mercy at this moment in this situation. I have said that it is not up to us to theorize how this may be brought about in detail. Yet, we are familiar with daily occurrences that may serve us as an example – or perhaps only a hint – to render the entrance of God's blessing into the universal order, as it affects us, plausible. Modern man is rather proud of his scientific achievements. Medicine, for instance, shows some spectacular accomplishments. Epidemics that formerly decimated entire continents have been wiped out. Formerly incurable diseases have been brought under control. Today's hopeless case may be treated tomorrow as a matter of unexciting medical routine. Shall we say that the surgeon or the physician is interfering with the laws of nature, since what was – because of the functioning of those laws – impossible yesterday is being accomplished today? What we have before us is a measure of coordination, on a human scale, between the realm of nature and that of the spirit. In free dedication to a self-imposed task, man accepts a challenge. He turns to the investigation of the laws of nature and finds that they are not as unequivocally committed to one course of action as he thought they might be. There is not just one road. There is a way and a bypass and a sidetrack. There is a law and a counter-law, a toxin and an antitoxin. One can intervene purposefully using nature to guide nature or even to defeat nature. This is the essence of all human control over nature, which the scientific man has gained. But what is available to man, should it not be accessible to his Creator? Of course, God is not a scientist; just because of that He may be able to accomplish no less than the ultimate scientist will ever be able to achieve, and He may be able to do so without having to revert to the method or the technique of science.

Let us consider a specific example. Assuming that in accordance with the laws of nature, a certain type of disease was indeed incurable; that there was indeed nothing in the universe which, if brought to bear on the sickness, could control and eliminate it. To pray to God for healing in such a case would be praying for a miracle. But if the sickness is curable, even if man may never succeed in discovering the cure, its cure by God's mercy would not imply any miraculous intervention with the universal order. Praying for such a cure would not be praying for a miracle but for the blessing of God to enter the order of nature here and now.

I believe that we are now in a better position to discuss the main theme of this chapter. The question is not whether prayers may be answered or are answered at all. The difficulty is presented by the rather disconcerting experience that so many of our prayers seem to fall on deaf ears, as it were. It may, however, be that an answer is granted much more often than we are aware of it. If normally one would pray for miracles to happen, the answer might be expected to be stark and convincing, for everyone to behold. However, since we pray for God's blessing within the natural scheme of human existence, who will say what shape God's blessing is to take? The answer may not be spectacular at all, yet it may nevertheless be a genuine divine response to our plea. In fact, one may discover an inclination in oneself to assume that God's *berakha* would not normally take on the form of the spectacular. God who spoke to Elijah was not in the wind nor in the earthquake, and not in the fire. He spoke to the prophet with "a still small voice." According to a talmudic dictum: "the blessing is found in what is hidden from the eye" (Taanit 5b). One ought to expect it to be so on the basis of the most significant feature of Jewish prayer. As we have seen, prayer in Judaism is not a crisis activity; it is part of the normal routine of daily life. For a Jew, living includes praying. The spectacular answer may be fitting for the spectacular occasion. A person who is about to drown and who is saved against all odds may well acknowledge his rescue as an answer to prayer. Such may be a visible divine response. The Jew, however, prays in acknowledgment of man's absolute dependence on God; he prays for understanding in the realization that all human understanding is from God; he prays for the daily bread and daily health, knowing that whatever his share may be, it is granted to him by God. He asks for divine protection, because without it he could not survive a single moment. Asking for God's blessings in such a mood, he does not look for spectacular answers to his prayers. However, he is sure with the conviction of faith that whatever he is and whatever he holds is due to the fact that at least some of his prayers are being answered all the time.

There are, of course, spectacular situations in the life of the Jew, and certainly no fewer than in the life of most people. What of the answers to our prayers in situations of crisis? Are they granted as often as one might expect them to be granted? When the question is put this way, one cannot help pursuing the thought further by asking: On what basis might one establish standards by which to determine, in advance, the frequency of the answers which could rightly be expected to such crisis praying? To pray correctly in a moment of real crisis – we understand it now fully – may not be easier than regular praying, but even more difficult. At a critical moment in human life, one is so preoccupied with the danger to oneself that the turning to God in prayer may itself be an act of despair, instead of one of faith and steady trust. One need not belittle even such prayer, even though one may see clearly how the situation which holds man within its grip may make it more difficult for him to move from preoccupation with himself, from self-confrontation, to confrontation with God. At such moments, in the very act of praying, a man may be still seeing only himself and his situation, and not turn really to face the Divine Presence. The situation of crisis is a great temptation for man to offer the *tefillat shav*, the prayer of futility, the prayer for the miraculous change of the laws of nature for our sake.

In full awareness of the difficulties of right praying in a situation of crisis, Judaism frees man from the prescribed obligatory prayer at such moments. Instead, one is taught to pray in the following manner: "Many are the needs of Your people Israel, but understanding they have little. May it be Your will, O Lord, our God, to grant each one sufficient for his livelihood, and to every creature in accordance with his need. Do for us what is good in Your eyes. Blessed are You who hears prayer" (*Mishneh Torah, Hilkhot Tefilla* 4:19).

Let us consider the implications of such a prayer. Whereas in the normal situation of daily existence, Jewish prayer articulates the needs of man in detail and asks for their fulfillment; in a situation of crisis, a Jew acknowledges in prayer his lack of understanding to know either what his needs are or in which way they could be best satisfied. When the danger is greatest, he leaves it all to God. The distinction between the two types of prayer is twofold. In the course of his normal daily life, a Jew may feel completely secure in his economic status, yet he will pray for livelihood; he may enjoy perfect health, nevertheless he will ask God for healing; he may be completely free from affliction and yet he will entreat God to spare him from affliction; he may be an intellectual giant, but he will plead for understanding; he may be a saint and ask for forgiveness. Because in this case he does not pray from a specific situation but from the existential one of man's absolute dependence on God, he knows what he needs. He needs life and everything that goes with it. He does not pray in a situation of preoccupation with a specific need. He is not about to die of hunger; he is not at this moment threatened by an enemy; he is not right now in the grip of some frightening disease. Just because of that, he elaborates the fundamental needs of his humanity. The elaboration is necessary because when one is not hungry, it is easy to forget that God is the Provider. When one is not sick, it is easy to imagine that one is not permanently in need of the Healer; when one is not afflicted, one is apt to take things for granted as if one were not forever dependent on the Redeemer.

But in a situation of actual crisis, one must pray differently. At such a moment, a man is overwhelmed by one specific need. His very life may be actually threatened. He is about to die of hunger, or he is about to be consumed by disease. The specific situation requires a specific remedy. Does he know what the remedy is? Can he spell it out in so many words? One of the commentaries on the code of Maimonides quotes the words of Rabbi Manoaḥ who, in explanation of the phrase *Hatov be'einekha aseh*, "Do to us that which is good in Your eyes," says: "Do not give us what appears good to us, for – who knows? – it may not be good at all in its ultimate outcome. We ask for what is good in Your sight, for that alone is perfectly good" (*Mishneh Torah, Hilkhot Tefilla* 4:19). When one finds oneself in acute danger, often one may not really know in what one's true salvation lies. Thus, in the crisis prayer of Judaism, man acknowledges his lack of understanding and pleads that God may take it from him in accordance with divine insight. It is obviously not necessary to elaborate on the manifold needs of human existence; at a time of crisis, it is unlikely that man will easily forget that he is a dependent creature and cannot go it all by himself. When one is at ease, Jewish prayer emphasizes the acknowledgment of man's perennial dependence on God for all of his needs; when one is actually in need, the emphasis is laid on trust in the goodness of God. A man with a great fortune to his name, who in daily prayer expresses his trust in the goodness of God who will not let him starve that day, is praying tritely. He cannot mean what he says. The right prayer for such a man is to come before God like a beggar and pleadingly acknowledge that all his economic security stems from God and has to be granted to him anew every moment of his life. If he can do this turning to God in all sincerity as if in the rags of one utterly destitute, he has indeed prayed. On the other hand, if in the throes of an emergency, in which a human being may find himself utterly helpless, he affirms his dependence on God, he may be doing what might be the easiest thing for him to do at the moment. It would still be prayer, but one of relatively little weight. However, if in full realization of the seriousness of the emergency he may face God and speak to Him in utter honesty: do unto me whatever is good in Your eyes, then he has prayed as one should.

Perhaps we may now understand better why it is so difficult to form an opinion about the frequency of God's answer, even when one might expect such answer to be more spectacular, as it ought to be in a definite crisis situation. Especially in such situations, if we pray rightly, we do not pray for miracles but for God's blessing. But the very nature of the situation is such that our wisdom is indeed inadequate to advise us unequivocally in what our good may consist. We may never know in what form God's blessing may reach us, especially when it is meant to be a response to a prayer of crisis. At times, God answers our prayers by refusing to grant us our request. In our lack of vision and understanding we may be praying against ourselves. Because of this, Rav, the great teacher of the Babylonian Talmud, prayed for "a life in which the desires of our heart are fulfilled for good," leaving the determination of what is good to God (Berakhot 16b).

There is, however, one other important consideration which may help us understand why the response to prayer may not be immediately convincing. The question, why God's answer is so seldom manifestly visible, cannot be separated from the much broader problem of theodicy, the problem that in our experience the righteous seems to be the afflicted one among men, whereas the wicked so often prosper. That prayer remains, seemingly, unanswered is a problem only if it refers to the prayer of the righteous. In our discussion thus far, I have analyzed the difficulties and requirements of right praying. We realize that there is no reason to expect prayer to be answered when it is not performed as it should be. Often, when we think we have not been answered, it may indeed be so. We have not been answered because we have prayed so as not to deserve to be heard. The unanswered prayer becomes a problem when it has been uttered by the righteous, when it is *tefillat yesharim*, prayer of the upright, of the man who in the act of praying has turned to God and has striven to imitate the divine attributes which make prayer possible. The problem exists only when the right prayer is not heard. As such it is a side issue of the classic quandary of all religious philosophy, that is, that of the righteousness of divine providence. He who can live in faith, notwithstanding the major problem, will easily accommodate himself to its side issue.

Far from having solved the problem of the theodicy, we believe that – elsewhere[1] – we have succeeded in showing that man could not exist as an ethically and spiritually responsible being, in a world in which the good would immediately and convincingly be rewarded, and evil punished with equal certainty. It is of the very essence of human responsibility that man may choose between various courses of possible action in freedom. Man could not be man if the challenge of choosing between good and evil were taken from him. However, it is exactly this choice that he would lose if doing good would always be rewarded, and doing evil would never remain unpunished. Man would act under the continuous threat of a Damocles' sword. The ethical and spiritual quality of his nature would be gone. Not dissimilar would be the consequences of a prayer which were always heard. Would it still be turning to God in faith and confidence if one were sure of the fulfillment of one's wishes every time one prayed? Would it still be a genuine attempt at imitating God if to be called by His name would in each case be the most promising enterprise in which to invest? The ways of God are mostly hidden from man; and so they must be in the case of prayer, too.

In midrashic and talmudic literature, the elective prayer is described in various ways. He who prays with *kavana*, for instance, may be sure that his prayer is heard. Rabbi Yehuda, the son of Rabbi Ḥiya, taught that he who occupies himself with the Torah, undeterred by conditions of hardship, his prayer is heard. On the other hand, Rabbi Ḥiya bar Abba said that he who prays again and again may know that his prayer is heard and God will do his will. One of the outstanding teachers of the Mishna maintained that he who practices charity and loving-kindness with his fellow men may rest assured that his prayer is accepted (Berakhot 32b).

1. Berkovits, *God, Man and History*, 143–57.

Needless to say, these are not contradictory opinions; they describe certain elements of prayer which will help it become right praying. All this, however, should be read in the light of a talmudic statement which may be considered fundamental for the understanding of the relationship of prayer and its answer. It is said that the prayer of the one who prays long "will not return empty."

However, it is also explained that this applies only to the man who does not look forward to being heard because he has prayed so well (Berakhot 32b). He who expects to be answered might as well brace himself for disappointment, for it is written: "Lengthy longing is a heartbreak" (Prov. 13:12). If a man prays long in order to be heard, the longness of his prayer will not improve but rather reduce its quality. If he prays again and again because he believes that thus he is more likely to find a more favorable reply, the more repetitious prayer will be the less meaningful one. If he practices charity so that the Almighty may be all the more impressed with him and, as a result, be inclined to fulfill his desires, his charity will be yet another form of self-seeking. Instead of assisting him in his prayer, it may impede its being granted. If one prays with *kavana,* one may be sure that one's plea is heard. But if one prays with *kavana* solely with the motivation that one's prayer be answered, the motivation itself destroys the *kavana.*

One cannot direct one's heart to God in order that one may succeed in the world. He who does so, directs his heart to the world and not to God. He prays with a false *kavana.* Man can only guide the concentration of his heart toward God for the sake of turning to God. The long prayer is valuable because it is long and sustained confrontation with God. Often-repeated prayers are significant because they represent man's continuous seeking out of God. One must pray well if one is to be answered, but one does not pray well if one prays in order to be answered. One should bring to God one's woes, trusting in His mercy; one should acknowledge one's dependence on Him when the need is least obvious; one should affirm one's faith in Him, relying on His goodness when trouble is greatest. All the time, one should seek Him.

This may be the secret of being heard: Yes, to ask because we are in need, but to turn to Him in our need because – when in need – we need Him most; yes, to hope that our prayer may be fulfilled, but to ask because in God alone we trust; to ask for health because – no matter what – He is the Healer; to plead for sustenance because He is the Provider, and there is none else; to implore Him for forgiveness because – no matter what happens to us – He is the Forgiver. Not what we ask for is important but that we ask God; that we turn to Him not because we are in trouble, but when in trouble, we turn to Him because God is the One to whom one turns. Of course, we desire to be heard. Similarly, we desire to live. Yet, we do not breathe in order to live, but live because we breathe. So we pray rightly not in order to be heard, but we are heard because we pray. We pray because man lives in the presence of God; because we desire to serve God with our very needfulness; because we serve Him with our hearts as we turn to Him in childlike trust as to the natural confidant of our innermost disappointments and longings. We do hope to be heard; but we pray because we seek His nearness, because we may pray to Him who is near. As to the rest, "Wait for the Lord silently, patiently" (Ps. 37:7); waiting for the answer, do not wait for what may be granted but for the One who alone may grant it; waiting for redemption, wait for the Redeemer.

The Prayer of the Martyrs

There are times when the gates of prayer seem to be closed, when even the prayers of the *tzaddikim* are powerless; times when all seems to be lost, when the doom impending becomes the doom inevitable, when the evil decreed becomes reality (Berakhot 61a). It is one of the rules of Jewish prayer that "man is obligated to bless God for the evil that befalls him as well as for the good that he receives" (Berakhot 54a). The insight on which this concept is based is derived from the words of the Bible: "You shall love the Lord your God with all your heart, with all your soul, and with all your might" (Deut. 6:5). The phrase "with all your soul" is interpreted as meaning "even if He takes your soul." The Jew does not minimize the evil and call it good. Evil is evil and good is good; and sorrow is not joy and joy is not sorrow. Does he then submit? Submission is an attitude of passivity; the service of God is the supreme human activity. There can be no human situation which is exempted from the service of the heart. In this service, at times, the heart itself may be required. At such moments, there is of course no room for supplication. All has been said; the case is closed and there is nothing to ask for. Is this the end of the confrontation, the end of prayer? On the contrary; when there is nothing to hope for, one hopes for God alone. When there is nothing to expect, one deals with God alone. It is then that the confrontation between God and man reaches its ultimate culmination. One may still make Him the confidant of one's sorrow, but instead of importuning, one accepts; instead of pleading, one praises.

Jews through the ages have incorporated this aspect of prayer in their lives. Whenever the heavy hand of destiny strikes irrevocably, the Jew stands up and prays, not for himself but for the sanctification of God's name and the establishment of His kingdom: *Yitgadal veyitkadash shemeh rabba*, "Magnified and sanctified be His name in the world which He has created, according to His will." However, no people on earth have practiced this kind of prayer as the Jews have on the numberless occasions of darkest martyrdom. When there was nothing to hope for, God was sufficient unto their untold millions. The prayers of Jewish martyrdom have been God's greatest triumph with man and man's incomparable triumph over the world.

The outstanding example of such prayer is that of Rabbi Akiva at the height of his martyr's death. They led him to his execution. As they were stripping the skin from his body alive, with combs of iron, he accepted upon himself the yoke of the kingdom of heaven, reciting the *Shema*. His disciples, however, interrupted him with the question: "Our master! Thus far?" Rabbi Akiva's answer was: "All my life long, I was perturbed by this verse which enjoins us to love God with all our soul, which means: even if He takes our soul. I said to myself: When will I have the opportunity to fulfill this commandment? Now that it has come to my hand, shall I not fulfill it?" (Berakhot 61a). What was it the disciples meant with their question? What was it Rabbi Akiva could have done? His life was forfeited. The execution was already in progress and there was no escape.

We believe that in such a situation the natural thing for a man to do might have been to storm the very gates of heaven in his agony, to cry to the God who has abandoned him, or to submit to the inevitable. Rabbi Akiva did neither of these. He was not even satisfied with accepting the will of God; he answered God's will with his own. With joy, he gave what was required of him – to love God with all his soul; in the supreme act of love, he gave himself. As he did so, he acknowledged: Hear, O Israel; the Lord our God, the Lord is the only One. Since the days of Rabbi Akiva, untold millions of Jews have concluded their lives with the same words on their lips, at the stakes of the Inquisition, during the Crusades, in the pogroms of Poland, Russia, Hungary, Romania, in the concentration camps of a Nazified Europe. Numberless are those, too, who through the ages were able to go and meet their Maker with joy, offering Him the love of all their souls. Rabbi Akiva's *Shema,* however, stands out as one that has perhaps never been paralleled. He recited the words not because he was about to die. From his own point of view, there was no drama about his acceptance of the yoke of the Kingdom of God. *Zeman Keriat Shema haya,* "It happened to be the hour for the prescribed recitation of the *Shema,*" says the Talmud. Ignoring the executioner and disregarding the agony of his body, Rabbi Akiva went on in his daily service of God as a matter of routine. He was performing the service of the heart as was his wont all the days of his life as required by each day. In the history of human martyrdom, there is nothing to equal the depth of the four Hebrew words: *Zeman Keriat Shema haya,* "It happened to be the hour for the recitation of the *Shema.*" In the entire history of the human race, there is no prayer on record that in breathtaking majesty and grandeur approaches even from afar the prayer of Rabbi Akiva.

We may appreciate the significance of the prayers of the martyrs in the light of Rabbi Akiva's prayer. Dare one say that in the prayers of the martyrs the relationship of God and man is reversed? When God gave Abraham the command to sacrifice his son Isaac, He said to him: *Kaḥ na et binkha,* which does not mean, as usually translated, "Take your son," but "please take your son" (Gen. 22:2). As it has been pointed out in the Talmud, "the Hebrew word *na* indicates a request" (Sanhedrin 89b). Subjecting Abraham to the supreme test of faith, God was asking him not to fail Him. Is not martyrdom always such a divine plea addressed to man? Normally, it is man who supplicates and God who answers; in the hour of the martyrs, it is – as it were – God who "supplicates" and man who responds. God can, of course, take as He pleases, but – at times – He wishes to receive. At times, in His unfathomable will, He asks for the love of "all the soul," as with Abraham, as with Rabbi Akiva and his colleagues in life as well as in martyrdom, as with all the martyrs of Israel. I have discussed earlier the concept of God's praying.

Normally, when man prays, God too "prays" that man may be called by His name and so may be answered. In the hour of the martyrs, it is God who pleads, but man too supplicates for the strength to be able to answer, so that God might be called by the name of those who sanctify Him, *Kedosh Yisrael,* the Holy One of Israel.

Section 2

Exile

In the Wilderness of the Nations*

Words which seem to apply very closely to the present situation of the Jewish people were once proclaimed by the prophet Ezekiel: "I will take you out from the nations; I will gather you in from the countries where you have been scattered; with a strong hand, with an outstretched arm, and with an outpouring of fury I will bring you into the wilderness of the nations, and I will enter into judgment with you there, face-to-face" (Ezek. 20:34–35). The future of Judaism may depend on our willingness to grasp fully the implication of these words.

God will bring His people out of the countries in which they have been scattered, and He will lead them not to salvation, not back to their Homeland – this will follow later – first He will lead them from all the countries of Jewish settlement into the Wilderness of the Nations. In

* Rabbi Berkovits delivered this sermon "during the darker days of the war," on Shavuot, in May 1942.

other words, Jewish settlements as they have emerged in the various countries of the world, Jewries as they have taken shape in the course of the long centuries of our history in exile in all corners of the world, will be broken up and dissolved; Jews and Jewries will be driven out into the Wilderness of the Nations.

Today, we have reached this stage in our history. The exiles have been exiled anew. Jewries all over the world have been uprooted. Those compact enclosures of Jewish life, each with a history of its own, each with a religious culture of its own suited to its environment, each almost a separate Jewish nation of its own, with distinct traditions and institutions, have been forced open and their contents poured out, spread out all over the world.

Think of Russian Jewry, of Polish Jewry, of German Jewry – they are no more. There are only former Russian, Polish, German Jews uprooted and wandering about in the Wilderness of the Nations.

Our whole people are in this situation. All of us. We like to think that American Jewry and English Jewry have been spared the tragedy of living in the wilderness. This is a misinterpretation of Jewish history. This would be true if the breaking up of the great historic Jewries were only a matter of migration, a matter of geography, of "whither," where to go, where to find a new home. Thank God, these questions and problems do not exist for the English and American Jewries. Materially at least and for the time being they are settled. And yet they too live in the wilderness. In fact, this tragic process of the breaking up of historic Jewries, of the disintegration of Jewish settlements, of banishment from the homes which Jews have found in the countries of the world and which in some cases they have inhabited longer than the present occupiers, into the homelessness of a new Exile, into the Wilderness of the Nations, started with the ancestors of those Jews who today constitute the bulk of the American and English Jewries. The tragedy began sixty, eighty, a hundred years ago, with the great migrations of Jews from Russia, Poland, Romania toward the West; it has culminated in our days in the breakdown of all the continental Jewries.

It is true that the material position of the Jewries in the Anglo-Saxon world is, thank God, much sounder than that of their brethren elsewhere. But this process of disintegration of the historic Jewries presents not only a problem of migration, of Jewish politics and economics; it involves a spiritual crisis of the first magnitude.

The disintegration of individual Jewries means in fact that Judaism is disintegrating. The shifting of the "Jewish Geography" brings in its wake the disorganization of the spiritual structure of Judaism. It is a mistake to think that Judaism can be transported – as it were – from one country to another. Judaism is not a book or a library which you may carry with you from one place to another. Judaism is not a mere theoretical system, a compilation of ideals and beliefs. Judaism is life lived by Jews, it is a system of purposes and intentions, carried into realization by living Jewries. The great Russian Jewry, with its own history, its own traditions, its Russo-Jewish propensities and idiosyncrasies, it was Judaism. In its dissolution Judaism also dissolves. Polish Jewry, German Jewry, in all their activities, their communal organizations and religious-cultural institutions, their particular style of thinking and living, represented various historic shapes of living Judaism. In their disintegration Judaism goes under, in their disappearance Judaism disappears.

One cannot replant the Judaism of one country in the soil of another. Every Jewry is unique. The shape that Judaism takes in the various Jewries is always "locally" determined. The Jewish emigrant always carries with him only the ruins of his former spiritual existence, the ruins of Judaism as lived in his own native Jewry, just as he carries in his little bundle the miserable remnants of his former material existence.

As soon as the Polish or Lithuanian Jew leaves his country he ceases to be the Polish or Lithuanian Jew. He becomes the former Polish or Lithuanian Jew. He becomes the shadow of the Polish or Lithuanian Jew, the shadow of a historic Jewish type. This is the real tragedy of the Jews who are forced out of the countries of their historic sojournings into the Wilderness of the Nations.

Let it be understood that I do not treat here only the recent refugees from the Continent. I deal with the Jewish situation in England and in America. For what else are the Jewish communities in the United Kingdom or in the United States, or South Africa, but the ghostly shadows of great Jewries, what else but the debris of the former Russian, Polish, and Lithuanian Jewries. Stop talking about English or American Jewry. There is no such thing as yet. There are Jews in these countries, but these countries have not yet become homes to new Jewries; they are still part of the Wilderness of the Nations into which Jews have been driven. There is no positive manifestation of Jewish life which could be called Anglo-Jewish. What is still Jewish with us is Russo-Jewish, Polish-Jewish, or Lithuanian-Jewish; and what English, is not Jewish, is often anti-Jewish, often the jettisoning of Judaism. Jews in the Anglo-Saxon world either vegetate on the remnants of former Judaisms imported by the emigrants, or else throw even such remnants overboard. "Anglo-Jewish" is an accident in Jewish history, not yet an achievement, as Russo-Jewish, Polish-Jewish, or German-Jewish was.

This, of course, is a hopeless situation which must lead to ultimate dissolution and extinction.

What can we do to avert the catastrophe that menaces us? This is not the place for developing a detailed plan of action. But we may try to indicate the goal toward which we must direct our endeavors. The first epoch in the modern history of Jews in Anglo-Saxon countries has reached its conclusion. It was the epoch of economic settlement in the new countries of Jewish emigration. While the struggle for proper economic conditions and social security lasted, the emigrants had to subsist on those remains of spiritual capital which they were able to save from the breakdown of the Jewries to which they originally belonged.

No longer are they emigrants today. Economically and politically they are settled in quite normal conditions. Materially they are already the children of a new age; spiritually, however, they live in a void. All they have are the fading memories of Vilna and Warsaw, of Kovno and Lodz. This is an impossible situation. The material resettlement of the remnants of former Jewries has been completed, as far as the Jews in the Anglo-Saxon world themselves are concerned. Now must follow the spiritual resettlement of Judaism in the cultural sphere of the English-speaking nations.

Now has the time come to create Anglo-Jewry as a new manifestation of a living Judaism; a Jewry that is Anglo-Jewish not because of the mere accident of geography or owing to its language, but in the sense that in it Judaism has found its own adequate expression in the midst of the Anglo-Saxon civilization. At the present crisis in Jewish history it will not do merely to follow the traditions of the past. It is our duty to create traditions for the future. Jews cannot forever continue to live in London, New York, Sydney, according to the "Minhag Polin"; the time has come when the "Minhag Britanya" or the "Minhag America" must be molded, or else we are lost. I do not wish to be misunderstood. I emphatically reject Reform or Liberalism. What I preach is historic Judaism.

The style of living of the new Jewries which are to be formed must be based on the foundations of the Jewish past; it must retain the intentions of our great religious culture, but it must relate Judaism to the rest of the world in the midst of which we have to live. In other words: Our task is not to imitate former Jewries, but to make Judaism real today; that is, with the help of the knowledge and the experience of the past to hammer out the religious-cultural shape of a new Jewry which shall emerge from the contact of Judaism with Anglo-Saxon civilization. Only when this task is performed shall we be redeemed from the Wilderness of the Nations.

Jewish Living in America

One of the most symptomatic facets of our Jewish life today is probably the appearance of a new type on the Jewish scene, that of the "good Jew." In this country, the percentage of people who seem to believe that they are "good Jews" must be exceedingly high. But the person who unabashedly proclaims himself a good Jew is a relatively new phenomenon in Jewish history. The pious and conscientious Jews of former generations never thought of themselves as "good Jews." In their minds the goal of Jewish living remained forever unrealized; and the further they advanced on the road of partial realization the more they were also aware of their own inadequacy and insufficiency. The truly revealing nature of this juxtaposition of two Jewish types is best appreciated as one notes how these differing forms of self-appraisal are accompanied by correspondingly differing attitudes toward the external, non-Jewish world around the Jew. In former generations, facing his own conscience the Jew was self-critical; standing before God he was conscious of his innumerable shortcomings; at the same time he was almost completely oblivious of the impression he made upon the outside world. For him, the decisive considerations were the requirements of living in accordance with the standards of Judaism.

On the other hand, the good Jew in his own eyes of our days is morbidly preoccupied with the task of making a good impression upon his Gentile surroundings. Thus he gives himself away: Judaism, by which he ought to live, he faces with self-righteousness; the society in which he lives, with self-consciousness. It is a sign of weakness. People who are reasonably sure of themselves, of their own worth, may afford being genuinely self-critical and in a healthy way indifferent to the opinions of others concerning them. Self-righteousness however is usually indicative of self-doubting, of a dim awareness of guilt unadmitted, and it goes naturally hand in hand with self-consciousness when facing others. The more one doubts one's own worth the more one is anxious to make a good impression on others. These are the paradoxical symptoms of moral insecurity.

To our mind, these symptoms are indicative of the fact that in the midst of the American Jewish community Jewish living is still in its problematic phase. There are Jews in America, there is a significant and valuable community of Jewish people, but Judaism has not yet been established in the New World. There is an American Jewry, but no American Judaism as yet.

Looked at from the angle of Jewish living, the American Jewish community is a Jewry of unsolved problems. They are all the problems of a new beginning in a new era and in a new world. Historically, American Jewry is still very close to the phase of its origin; spiritually it is still largely an Immigration Jewry. The most lasting effects of all immigration are to be found in the psychological unsettling of the human personality. As the immigrant changes his geographical bearing, he also tears himself away from an established order of living in which he had his spiritual and cultural roots. The experience usually throws into disorder the traditional concepts and practices which made up the historically grown pattern of life in the old familiar world of the wanderer. Immigration is essentially inimical to tradition; it works as a solvent upon historically established forms of living as well as upon an accepted order of values.

But Jewish living represents just such a system of behavior; one determined by a historic tradition and reflecting a scale of values which has been passed on from generation to generation. The disintegrating force of immigration has been pounding away at the traditional forms of Jewish life and thus American Jewry started out on its course in Jewish history while engulfed by the advancing dissolution of the historic essence of Jewish living. In this connection one must also take into account the consequences of the new rhythm of work and endeavor which is so often forced upon the immigrant by the practical demands of his economic resettlement in the new land. Especially in the first generation the struggle for existence is grim and requires all the energies of a man; the need for bread, a home, clothing, is commanding and it can often not be met without the surrendering of traditional forms of Jewish living like the observance of the Sabbath and other holy days. The further dissolving effects of such surrender upon the culture of the Jewish home and Jewish family life in general is incalculable; but the change in living practice is facilitated by the psychological upheaval of the very process of immigration, which unsettles and confuses the traditional world of the immigrant. The psychological upheaval makes it easier for him to acquiesce in the new rhythm of life forcefully suggested to him by the economic struggle for survival; and thus the process of disintegration of traditional forms of Jewish living is accelerated. The psychological change in mentality and the economically conditioned change in living practice, reinforcing each other, create an almost vicious circle of dissolution.

So handicapped, the new American Jewry came into being in a new era of human history. The late nineteenth century and early decades of the twentieth, which saw the main waves of Jewish mass migration to the American continent, have witnessed revolutions and wars on a global scale, an almost universal transformation in the material technique of living as well as in the mental attitude of man. The spirit of the age, dominated to a large extent by the scientific approach to the questions and problems of man, was experimental, critical, and almost passionately unfriendly toward the historical and traditional. The conflict between the new spirit of the times and the historic religions remained unresolved and its consequences spread into the consciousness of the broad masses of the entire human race, undermining their loyalty to traditional concepts of order and action. Ever since the Jewish people left the ghettos in Europe, they in their turn became more and more involved in the conflict and felt its repercussions. But the long-established Jewries of Europe, in their homes and institutions, in communal consciousness and the momentum of organized Jewish living rooted deeply in many centuries of experience and practice, possessed rich resources of historic faith and substance that enabled them to keep the invading forces of the new age at bay, hoping not without justification that one day the problems posed would be solved and thus the rebellious spirit of the new era itself absorbed in the historic order of Jewish living.

In America however, to the generation of immigrant Jews fell the unenviable task of building a new Jewry that in order to be Jewish in the spiritual and cultural-religious sense of the word had to incorporate in its fundamental structure historically evolved standards of values and traditionally hallowed practices of living; the task had to be undertaken at a most unpropitious moment in the spiritual history of mankind: historicity was breaking down the world over, mankind was turning its back on the past, experiment took the place of tradition. The individual experience of the immigrant, resulting from the psychological and economic revolution in his own narrow personal life, was fortified by the experience of the entire human race, following in the wake of very similar transformations on a universal scale: all around him the traditional order of living was going to pieces and a truly new era was afoot.

As if further to exacerbate the situation from the angle of Jewish living there was also the problem of adjustment. It might almost be called the problem of America, because it is unique in the history of Jewish migration and results from the nature of American life and American civilization. If American Jewry is one of the youngest in Jewish history, American civilization is the latest in the history of great civilizations. It has not so much grown out of the past as it was consciously created by people breaking with the past. Compared with the civilization of Europe, America's is experimental and untraditional, it is more future-oriented and much less past-burdened. It is young; it is the child of the new era; and the spirit of the New World could not but make its impact upon the immigrants from the old one. When Jews went from Poland or Russia to England, for example, they met with a mentality imbued with a sense of history, they came face-to-face with a civilization that was traditionally anchored; the surrounding world itself suggested the organizing of Jewish life along traditional lines. In America the suggestive power of the surroundings worked in the opposite direction, proposing self-reliance in the pursuit of happiness rather than leaning heavily on the historic experience of the group. The experimental attitude toward life and its meaning breaks down the group consciousness and dissolves the sense of belonging to a historic community.

In keeping with its own *raison d'être,* the spirit of American civilization tends to atomize the historic consciousness of an immigrant community, thus drawing its individual members into its own stream until they are fully assimilated. Never before in the history of the Jews has assimilation been so easy and also so tempting as in America. The civilizations of the Old World were mostly exclusive toward minorities or newcomers; neither did they have the moral excellence to make them, for their own sake, a desired form of life for minority groups. Jewish assimilation in Europe was mainly a policy of escape from the consequences of Jewish living. Of course, it had to face the heartbreaking irony that in his endeavor to escape the assimilationist Jew had to embrace a ruling civilization that in its treatment of minorities was sufficiently inhuman to make escape desirable. In America, however, the fugitives from the burden of Europe found a civilization that was anxious to receive and to assimilate the newcomer, that in its own right deserved to be respected and loved for its generous humanity and spirit of freedom. And again I observe how the various elements present in the new situation work hand in hand against the successful ordering of a system of Jewish living: the atomization of the historic group consciousness of the immigrant community is accompanied by the invitation to assimilate to a friendly, freedom-loving civilization.

To complicate matters still further there is also the problem of belonging, following intrinsically from the nature of a civilization of freedom. In most countries of Jewish settlement in the past, the organic Jewish community was also a legal organization, officially recognized by the state. In most European countries, the Jew was born into the community and the community as such had a certain amount of jurisdiction over him; he belonged automatically. If he resented the authority of the community he had to disaffiliate himself by a formal declaration of non-belonging. Since only very few were ready to perform an act that was tantamount to desertion, the overwhelming majority of Jews belonged to the community and – in one way or another – actually contributed to the maintenance and safeguarding of organized Jewish life. Not so in

America, a country that prides itself – and rightly so – on its religious freedom. The organic community as such, if it exists at all, has no legal status; belonging must be expressed by an act of voluntary affiliation. The individual Jew must decide to belong and thus build and strengthen the community by his free decision. At the same time his desire to belong to the historic community of his origin has been considerably undermined by a rich measure of freedom from historic ties, brought about by immigration in an era of transformation, as well as by the political freedom of America inviting assimilation.

These then were the manifold ramifications of the problem of the new beginning that were involved in the creation of American Jewry; and they are still with us, still unresolved. As a result, the traditional or historic forms of Jewish living have been caught in a process of continually advancing disorganization and the vacuum thus created has been invaded by living practices based on the one-day wisdom of newspapers and magazines, on mass-produced thinking and streamlined feeling, on the standards and taste of the motion picture industry and the values of the TV screen. Unfortunately, many an American Jew is prepared to see in a situation which is the result of unsolved problems the positive expression of the new American Jewish way of life: the historically problematic is accepted as the timely valid order of things. The "good Jew" of our days is the product of such acceptance. He is the expression of a philosophy that has been devised to justify as a matter of principle, and to elevate to a form of living, what is essentially the perplexity of a generation. Since however we cannot for long escape the feeling that in reality we have embraced a sham, we react with internal self-righteousness, only to betray our moral insecurity in the next moment as we face the world around us with sickly self-consciousness.

The question which must be put at this juncture is, of course, how then are we to grapple creatively with a situation of such complexity. It would appear to us that there are a number of avenues of approach which might be profitably pursued. Having discussed the conflict between the critical and experimental spirit of the age and the historic forms of Jewish living as well as the toll the conflict took on Jewish living, one ought to add that the moment is ripe now for restoring the balance. What I have called the spirit of the age is itself involved in an internal crisis. It has obviously overreached itself; the international unrest, confusion of standards, and chaos of living practice indicate that the forces which it unleashed have not been mastered by it.

As its limitations become more and more manifest, one appreciates with ever-increasing clarity that the scientific attitude had claimed for itself a preeminence in life which was not due to it on the basis of intrinsic merit. The mesmerizing spell which the spirit of the scientific era once was able to cast over man has spent itself by now. The entire intellectual equipment of this epoch must now be subjected to critical scrutiny. From the angle of a comprehensive philosophy of living only questions have been asked but no positive answers found. Judaism, representing a comprehensive philosophy of life and living, may now well come into its own again. Of course, a great deal of original scholarly work has to be done on the body of Judaism itself; a sustained and comprehensive effort of creative reinterpretation is required. In the light of the new issues of human inquiry and concern, which have been raised by the spirit of science and historical criticism, new facets of Jewish teaching must be raised into eminence making the Jewish philosophy of living relevant for our generation. This can be done today, but it ought to be done according to a broad-visioned plan and with enthusiastic perseverance. Original Jewish scholarship must be encouraged and supported, existing institutions of higher Jewish learning strengthened, and the results of such new scholarship and learning popularized and made easily accessible.

That an intensive educational system, to embrace practically all age groups, is vital is, of course, a truism. But planning and conducting our educational activities on all levels we must bear in mind that the historic consciousness of American Jewry is weak; the community as such is lacking a strong sense and experience of Jewish historicity. One of the aims of the educational process must be to bring about a persistent and intimate confrontation between the American Jew and Judaism as a great historic civilization. But in order to achieve that one must go back to the sources. A gradual return to the sources of Judaism alone will enable us to recover our lost sense of historic consciousness. Infinitely more important than the imparting of mere knowledge about Judaism is the confrontation with the original inspiration of the Jewish genius.

Without a restored historic consciousness, flowing into the body politic of American Jewry through the contact with the original sources of creative Jewish inspiration, a genuine appreciation of Judaism is hardly possible. But Jewish education that fails to impart appreciation of Judaism is worthless. Only he who appreciates Judaism can be led to desire it and only he who desires it will wish to belong to the community that lives by it. At this juncture, the primary aim of all Jewish education must be exactly this, to educate the desire for and to create the will to Judaism.

The will to Judaism has the most important bearing on Jewish living. For Jewish living is of course not identical either with Jewish scholarship or with the appreciation of Judaism as a historic civilization; it is not the same as the faith of the Jew or the intellectual acceptance of Jewish ideals. Jewish living is what the words themselves indicate, the practice of Judaism. The term takes its meaning from Jewish history. Historically speaking, Jewish living of course stands for a pattern of behavior as prescribed by Judaism. It does mean the observance of the Sabbath and other festivals, it does call for the observance of dietary laws, it does include a system of religious practices. With whatever new significance the one or the other group within Jewry may wish to invest the term, the principle of historic continuity must be safeguarded. Any interpretation that discards the principle of historic continuity in this context, actually rejects the very essence of the idea of Jewish living. It is true that there are problems of religious observance resulting from the rhythm and tempo of American life; those problems constitute a challenge to the halakha and its teachers. But however difficult the practice of Judaism in a given situation may be, Jewish living can mean but one thing: the doing of Judaism, its practice and observance. And even today, with many of the practical problems of Jewish living still unsolved, there remain relatively ample opportunities for Jewish living; there is the Jewish home, many aspects of Sabbath observance are realizable even by the Jew who works on the Sabbath, and many others. But the essential is the will to Judaism. Jewish living itself must be wanted and desired. No disciplined behavior and practice is possible where the will for it is lacking.

We must however appreciate that when all is said and done a residue in the problem of Jewish living in America will forever be found irremediable. Jewish living is the manifestation of a comprehensive civilization that exists in its own right. But economically, politically, and to a large extent, also culturally, American Jewry lives in closest affiliation with American civilization and indeed is a constituent part of it. While the American Jew may well create a valuable symbiosis between the principle value concepts of American civilization and those of Judaism, the rhythm of living practice between two self-contained civilizations can hardly ever be synchronized. For example, the Sabbath as a day of Jewish living is ideally placed in the context of a civilization that in all its ramifications rests on that day; but its irrelevance within the framework of a civilization that rests on the Sunday can never be fully eliminated. At best, the complete observance of the Sabbath is an act of considerable self-sacrifice. This discrepancy in the practical life rhythm between the two civilizations is the cause of the irremediable residue of the problem of Jewish living in America. Nevertheless, radical changes in the pattern of Jewish living carried out as a matter of principle, the setting up of an American *Shulḥan Arukh* as it were, are certainly not justifiable for the sole reasons of practical considerations. American Jewry is not the only Jewry in the world. And if in the dilemma of Jewish living in America we have discovered an insoluble residue let us recognize it for what it is, viz. the *galut* of Judaism.

The American Jew may sincerely believe that politically he no longer lives in the Diaspora; his practical inability to fully realize Jewish living ought to bring home to him the truth that even on the American continent the *Shekhina* remains in exile. In the rise of the State of Israel history itself points to the adequate place for Jewish living, the natural home of Judaism. Not that there are no problems of Jewish living in the Jewish state; but there the possibility of realization is complete and there is no *a priori* problem of insolubility. This, however, shows why radical changes in the halakha of Jewish living, dictated solely by the practical difficulties of the American Jew must be to no avail. The "irremediable residue" being the direct result of *galut*, it can certainly not be treated by the radical method of cutting through the Gordian knot. The obstinate resistance of the *galut* to being completely ignored cannot be reduced by a change in the provisions of the halakha or through a revision of Jewish philosophy or theology. The only solution to the *galut* is *geula*, redemption.

Let us with humility accept the fact that Jewish living in America is not fully realizable rather than to elevate a failure to a principle of living. It may afford us some comfort to know that the problem of Jewish living in the State of Israel is no less serious than it is in America, that indeed there are some obvious similarities in the situation in both countries. Since obviously, a more complete solution is feasible in the natural homeland of Judaism, American Jewry, too, is bound to benefit by the solutions reached there. I do not suggest that we rely on the Jewish people of the Jewish state to provide the remedy; there is no guarantee to be offered that they will be more successful than we. The problem of the insoluble residue that we have recognized as the *galut* of Judaism in our life directs our attention to our brethren in Eretz Yisrael and the rest of the world; it enjoins us to work with them hand in hand as we seek the solution to the problem of Jewish living in a new era and in a new world.

Toward Jewish Authenticity

One of the most revealing symptoms of the fundamental transformation in the Jewish history of our generation is the fact that today's active Jewries are all young. Although we are about to celebrate American Jewry's tercentenary, only about seventy years ago there were less than a quarter of a million Jews in the United States.[1] The bulk of the Jewries in the Anglo-Saxon world is still made up of the immigrants themselves and their children of the first or second generation. The situation is the same in the Latin American countries and, of course, our observation is even more correct when applied to that youngest of Jewries, the Jewish people in the State of Israel. Today we are left with "Immigration Jewries" alone. It is a most unusual development even in the turbulent history of our people and its full appreciation is a basic requirement for the understanding of contemporary Jewish life as well as for the planning of its future.

The term "Immigration Jewry" does not only refer to the accidents of Jewish migrations; it is also indicative of the intimate structure – or its

1. In 1654, the first Jews arrived in New Amsterdam. In 1954, American Jews celebrated their 300th anniversary with hundreds of celebrations, conferences, and publications. On this, see Arthur Goren, "A 'Golden Decade' for American Jews, 1945–1955," *Studies in Contemporary Jewry* 8 (1992): 3–20.

lack – of a young Jewish community. An Immigration Jewry is one that has not yet succeeded in establishing its claim to historic authenticity. Whether a Jewry is an authentic one, or not, I believe may be recognized by the nature of its problem of survival. The problem of survival seems to be perennial with Israel. But it has accompanied us in two essentially different versions. The threat to Jewish survival may come from without, as the result of external intolerance and persecution; or it may emanate from internal weakness, causing disintegration from within.

With the great Jewries of the past, whose historic legitimacy no one will doubt, survival was always an external problem, imposed by the enmity and hatred of the Gentile world. But none of these Jewries ever had to contend with a problem of survival following from its own inadequacy. Their religious and cultural future was never in doubt on account of the insufficiency of the spirit. There were always problems, but Judaism itself was never problematic or in doubt. In an authentic Jewry, Judaism's vitality is such a natural phenomenon that a Jew is as little aware of this vitality as a healthy body is consciously aware of its health. Among the Jews of Poland, Lithuania, Hungary, and Romania, prior to the Second World War, they would discuss antisemitism, and its many disabilities. They would strive for a solution of "the Jewish problem." However, a problem of the survival of Judaism due to the religious-spiritual weakness of the Jews themselves never entered the mind; it did not exist.

With an Immigration Jewry the problem of survival is acute in the reverse sense. Externally, as a threat of persecution and oppression, it is hardly present. This of course is what one would expect. The very essence of all migration is to escape conditions of insecurity; people do not move from one house of bondage to another. On the other hand, the very upheaval of emigration disorganizes the established order of Jewish living, it undermines formerly accepted values and it poses the problem of the adequate forms of Judaism in the new surroundings. Internal weakness seems to follow in the wake of the migratory waves, there is a temporary eclipse of Jewish creativity and a lack of Jewish faith; clarity is wanting in vision and firmness in purpose; survival becomes a problem because of threatening disintegration from within. It is this internal problem of Jewish survival that characterizes

Immigration Jewries. It pursues them in a twofold sense: biologically as well as spiritually. Immigration Jewries rely even biologically on "imported" Jewish substance; they have as yet not established their ability to guarantee the perpetuation of that substance. But they are even less established spiritually. With them the future of Judaism itself is at bay.

The problem of creative survival – and there is no other – is the uppermost problem of the Anglo-American Jewries; and it has not been solved yet for the State of Israel either. Authentic Jewries, whose ability to perpetuate themselves both biologically and spiritually requires no affirmation, produce no philosophies of survival; "survivalism" is unknown in their midst. The ugly word is the ugly symptom of Immigration Jewries whose ability of self-perpetuation is still problematic.

It is however well not to confuse Immigration Jewries with assimilationist Jewries. To be sure, assimilationist Jewries too are lacking natural vitality. But with them self-immolation is the conscious policy and Jewish survival more of a threat to be escaped than a problem to be solved. The problematics of Immigration Jewries are the result of historic developments over which the Immigration Jew has but little control. If Immigration Jewries are not as yet authentic, their problems are authentic problems of Jewish history and as such must be treated with all the seriousness and dedication and with the utmost humility of which we are capable. Assimilationist Jewries are the refuse of Jewish history; Immigration Jewries are its invaluable seeds. Whatever the next epoch will bring for Judaism and the Jewish people, it will come from these new Jewries. Their problems are therefore the genuine problems of Judaism and their possibilities, our only promise for the future.

If the specific nature of its survival problem is the mark by which a Jewry may be classified, let us see what are the significant positive features of those Jewries which we recognize as authentic. As we take stock of Babylonian, Spanish, medieval Central European, Polish, Russian, and German Jewries, I note that, despite their undoubted legitimacy, in many ways they differ from each other. Babylonian Jewry's talmudical interpretation of Judaism is certainly different from the philosophical and poetic approach developed with such ingenuity and grace by Spanish Jewry.

Similarly, Judaism in the Judeo-Arabic garb was far removed from the somber, almost "puritan" Judaism of a Rashi or the Tosafists of the Middle Ages, completely circumscribed by "the four ells of the halakha." And so one might continue tracing the differences of German, Polish, and Russian Jewries closer to our own times. Each of these Jewries revealed a bent of its own in intellectual emphasis, in emotional experience and its evaluation; each one had a characteristic tendency in its interpretation of the meaning of life, in its analysis of human nature and of man's relationship to God. It is probably the most significant aspect of all these differences that they were not brought about by conscious disagreements in matters of theology or dogma. The Jew in Babylon, Spain, Germany, and Poland would adhere to the same tenets of Judaism and yet, in each one of these historic types Judaism found new expression. They were all legitimately rooted in Judaism and expressed the essence of their life through it. Their differences were conditioned by the accidents of the time and place in which they developed. Judaism is the form of life of a living society, and so it is involved in the web of all life; it is related to everything that lives with it and around it. It is conditioned by everything that lives and strives in this world and is of course conditioning everything in its turn. While it is acted upon, it also acts and reacts. Judaism has its anchorage in eternity, in facts, values, and goals of enduring consequence and significance; its historic path in time and space, however, cannot be severed from the accidents of time and space.

The broader web of life, of which Judaism cannot but be a part, colors its entire structure. The chain of action and reaction between itself and the world about it changes according to cultural, sociopolitical, and economic conditions. As a result, different facets of Judaism are spelled out in history, and different forms of Judaism emerge. There is no self-contained existence in this world. Nothing that lives can escape contact with life around it. Every culture is some form of a "symbiosis" – be it positive or negative – with the rest of all that is. And so it has been with Judaism too all through history. The operation of this inescapable principle of involvement with all life has produced the many different Jewries. They are all authentic and yet individually distinctive to the extent that one may lay down the rule: *every authentic Jewry is unique*. The various historic Jewries are a good illustration of the truth that history never repeats itself.

Since uniqueness is conditioned by time and place it may easily degenerate into mere compromise with and, finally, assimilation to the surrounding culture or civilization. In the authentic Jewries this tendency is corrected by unqualified Jewish identification. Notwithstanding their uniqueness, they were related in essential unity. Whether they were contemporaneous but established in different countries, or whether the one knew the other only across the long-stretched vistas of time, they always lived with an awareness of the all-pervading common peoplehood of Israel, as one in history and one in the world. In spite of their distinctive marks, whatever happened to the one was felt by the other, for indeed they were one in body. Whatever was created by the one, was accepted by the other, for they were one in spirit. Spanish Jewry was *unique*, but its tragedy was a *universal* Jewish tragedy, just as Yehuda HaLevi and Maimonides, though typically "Sephardim," belong to all Israel. A Jewry that is unique but to such an extent that it has lost its anchorage in the substratum of Jewish peoplehood and Judaism, which is common to all Jewries, is empty of Jewish essence; on the other hand, any Jewry in whose midst identification with the past or with other Jewries, or with already established expressions of Judaism, is so intense that it leaves no room for the development of its own individuality, is bound to be stagnating – a Jewry without a future. Uniqueness, which distinguishes each Jewry, and the essential unity that embraces them all, are contradictory tendencies which keep each other in check. These opposing tendencies result in a tension which is the source of the authentic Jewish dynamism. The need for individuality renders identification (with all other Jewries and with every other legitimate expression of Judaism) creative; and identification in its turn safeguards the authenticity of the newly emerging individuality.

Bearing these considerations in mind, what follows for a situation in which we are left with Immigration Jewries alone? How do we move to renewed authenticity? In the light of what has been said, we may better appreciate the mistakes we have made and clarify the direction we ought to follow. If our Immigration Jewries are to become authentic they will have to be unique; the authenticity of their uniqueness, however, will have to emerge from their unqualified identification with all Israel and with all Judaism in all times and in all places.

It is not possible to establish in America the replica of another Jewry, formerly in existence in another part of the world, however valuable that Jewry might have been. It was the mistake of early Orthodoxy in this country that it attempted to build Judaism in the image of Polish, Russian, and Hungarian Jewries. There was indeed full identification, but no appreciation of the vital need of uniqueness, which – as we have seen – always results from the particular "setting" in which a Jewry finds itself in history. The mistake was probably unavoidable, but its cost was high. Especially with the youth, the most time-and-place-conditioned section of any community, Orthodoxy became associated with the Old World; it was the Judaism of "Zaide" and "Bubbe." Young Jews recognized it for what it was: an attempted copy of Old World Jewries. As such it did not concern them. It is doubtful whether to this day official Orthodoxy in this country understands what is implied in the inescapable necessity of making American Jewry *authentic* yet *unique*.

We do not mean to suggest that early Reform Judaism appreciated the challenge of the situation. The attempted transplantation of German Reform to the American scene was absurd. It "thrived" only because, unfortunately, Orthodoxy could not master the situation. However, one might concede that today certain forms of Reform, as well as Conservatism, do represent expressions of Jewish life which are unique, i.e., conditioned mainly by the nature of American civilization. It is however doubtful to what extent they are authentic. They seem to be failing in the essential test for the authenticity of all uniqueness: they lack the almost instinctive sense of oneness with everything that has gone before them and exists about them in the history and reality of Israel. The unqualified identification with Rabbi Akiva, Maimonides, Rabbi Yosef Karo, the Gaon of Vilna, with the Lubavitcher Hasid living next door, is missing. It is for this reason that the uniqueness which we behold in American Jewry is not yet creative. Since it is lacking authentic Jewish essence, its uniqueness does not establish individuality and its survival value is more than dubious.

If we look at another one of the Immigration Jewries, the population of the State of Israel, our analysis becomes even more pertinent. The conditions, the tasks, the problems, and the responsibilities with which Israel confronts us are unparalleled in the history of our people. Israel in the State of Israel possesses of course much more convincing signs of uniqueness than any other contemporary Jewry. What is more, its uniqueness is apparently genuinely Jewish: the Hebrew language, political independence, the ancient homeland, etc. Nevertheless, even in Israel identification, as used in this context, must be the acid test of the authenticity of uniqueness. In spite of "Ivrit" and Hebrew culture and political sovereignty, without complete identification with all historic Israel and all historic Judaism, uniqueness cannot be the legitimate expression of Jewish life. Of course, identification may easily be turned into a purely national idea, as an element of national unity. And one might argue that in no Jewry is the sense of national identification with all Israel more intensive than in Eretz Yisrael. We are however not justified in taking it for granted that such will be the case for all times to come. Without spiritual identification, the ties of national unity itself are bound to weaken. The small but very active group of the "New Canaanites," who see in Israeli Jewry a new people and reject any connection with the "foreign" Jews of the Diaspora, is a danger signal that indicates the direction in which even a Hebrew-speaking Jewry may move when uniqueness is not authenticated by spiritual identification.

All major contemporary Jewries are still in the phase of "Immigration" because nowhere have we as yet succeeded in combining the need for distinctive individuality with the necessity for embracing identification. The dynamism that is due to the tension between these two opposing requirements is as yet hardly existent among us. There is no tension: those who are for authenticity do not grasp the aspect of uniqueness without which no Jewry can ever exist, while those who insist on uniqueness care little for authenticity, without which no Jewry will ever survive. Without this dynamism, there is no creativity. In the circumstances, Orthodoxy, the guardian of the essence of Judaism, will stagnate, while the Reformers and secularists, who urge time-conditioned individuality, will be without essence. Unfortunately, time is not on our side. Immigration Jewries, unformed as they are, are wide open to the inroads of assimilation and drifting estrangement. The transformation of Immigration Jewries into new authentic ones is a revolutionary undertaking, which cannot be carried out with formulae that have been conceived for the normal functioning and preservation of already established Jewries. It is for this reason that all the inherited "brands" of Jewish philosophy have become irrelevant. Orthodoxy, Reform, Conservatism, Zionism – they all miss the vital issues of our generation.

In order to meet the challenge of our times effectively, we must find new formulae and discover new approaches. They are all there within Judaism, waiting for us to be lifted into the light of a new day in our history. In order to accomplish our task, we need no less scholarship than there existed among the Old World Jewries but scholarship of a more imaginative and more creative nature; not less adherence to *mitzvot maasiyot,* but a practice of Judaism which is well integrated with the world in which Jews live; not less love for Judaism, but a more adequate interpretation of its importance for the twentieth-century scene. Finally, we need not less *yirat Shamayim* than past generations of Jews called their own, but rather the kind that is informed by love and respect for these Jewries of immigration, called into the chaos of a new beginning by overwhelming historic upheavals. Their perplexities are genuine problems of Judaism and they must be accepted and helped and guided. What we need is *yirat Shamayim* that is humble and sincere enough to be justified in taking risks, and bold and visionary enough to be able to do so, for the sake of Heaven – risks of the spirit as well as of the deed.

The *Galut* of Judaism

Discussion of the relationship between the State of Israel and the Diaspora seems in increasing measure to elicit from American Jews the opinion that America is no *galut* and American Jewry no part of a global diaspora. American Jews are citizens of the United States, equal in status and loyalty to the members of any other denomination or racial group. Speaking politically, this may well be so. The civic and political position of the Jew in this country has certainly very little in common with the one he used to hold in the countries of discrimination and persecution. It is very likely that America will never sink to the level of a Germany or a Poland. It is, however, seldom realized that the question retains its significance far beyond the realm of civic and political affairs. Whether life outside Eretz Yisrael is exile or not cannot be decided on the basis of one's citizenship alone; the issue affects the very essence of Judaism.

It should not be difficult to see the point, especially as one recalls – but alas, as we usually do not – that the question at hand has actually nothing to do with the coming into being of the Jewish state. For many centuries, Jews the world over considered themselves living in exile; generation after generation hoped and prayed for the return to Zion. To believe in the coming of the Messiah was an essential mark of Jewishness. Therefore, at any time, even before the establishment of the State of Israel, the question was no less appropriate than it is today: Is

America *galut* or not? If, thanks to American democracy and the Constitution of the United States, the answer is that American Jewry is not living in exile, then this must have been so in, say 1855, no less than in 1955. Neither the question nor its solution have anything whatsoever to do with the existence of a Jewish state.

Only when the issue is seen in this context is one in a position to analyze its internal Jewish significance. Since the rejection of *galut* status on the part of a Jewish community does not hinge on the establishment of "Israel," it is obvious that the refusal to acknowledge political loyalty to that state does not dispose of the question. Its true significance today is the same as it might have been at any time before 1948. Any German Jew, for example, who in the nineteenth century maintained that Germany was no exile was not only making a statement on the nature of his citizenship but was also offering a Judaism of his own. If German Jewry was not part of a Jewish diaspora – as so many of them sincerely believed – then naturally all references to Zion and to the future return of the Jewish people to their ancestral land, with which religious literature and observance were replete, became meaningless and the entire structure of Judaism itself had to be remolded without them. In this regard nothing much has changed since the days of so-called "classical" Reform. If America is no *galut,* Zion and the rich connotations of the idea lose their traditional and historic meaning for the American Jew. He will hardly be able to read the Bible in an unexpurgated edition. With the elimination of Zion as the goal toward which Jewish history is moving, the worldview and the philosophy of history of the prophets, intrinsically linked to their theology and concept of Israel, will also go by the board. What is left is a vague universalistic message, specifically conceived to suit a particular situation and not altogether dissimilar to that accepted by Christian theology. Whatever value such allegorical interpretation of the original prophetic word may otherwise possess, it can no longer be called Jewish in the light of the historical meaning of that term. Therefore, the question whether America is or is no *galut* is not one of momentary significance; it is not validly related to the existence of the State of Israel. It must be considered in the context of the meaning of Judaism and the entire range of Jewish history.

To hold that a Jewry, outside Eretz Yisrael, is not in exile implies that any country with a high level of freedom and democracy may be a home not only to Jews but to Judaism as well. Obviously, such an opinion calls for a corresponding interpretation of Judaism itself, one which posits that, given favorable political conditions, Judaism is realizable anywhere in the world. This interpretation, however, cannot be maintained without drastically revising what has been historically established as the very essence of Judaism. One of the most revealing aspects of that essence is to be recognized in the tradition that Abraham was not the founder of a religion or the fountainhead of a church but the father of a people. What differentiated him from the home and the land in which he was born and reared was the nature of his faith and the way of life it implied. That faith and that life served as starting points for the formation of a new people. This tradition does not mean to convey the notion that Abraham's faith and his fatherhood of Israel were merely coincidental. The faith necessarily leads to the people because it requires active implementation in life. The faith interprets life in its entirety and obligates man to action in conformity with itself in all spheres of life.

Judaism is thus all-embracing in its application: it has its own concepts of the value of the individual, the nature of the family, the function of society; it has its own philosophy of religion and ethics, its own standards of justice and mercy. The belief and the ideology may be that of an individual; the implementation with reference to the whole of life can only be accomplished by the group. Only the group that wields a measure of control over its own destiny sufficient to enable it to order the varied manifestations of its life in accordance with such an all-encompassing faith is in a position to realize Judaism as a whole. To the extent to which such control and authority are lacking, Judaism remains unrealizable. But realization is essential to Judaism and the group that may most completely achieve it is a people sovereign in its own home. Judaism is not nationalism, but the implementation of its worldview requires a measure of sovereign peoplehood as a minimum basis and necessary instrument for implementation. Outside the Jewish land, vast aspects of Judaism remain locked in the prison of abstract theory. For instance, the *Ḥoshen Mishpat,* comprising the judiciary system, is without applicability; the *Even HaEzer,* regulating marriage and family life, becomes relevant to so limited a degree that what is left of it is almost inextricably entangled in a web of problems which are hardly soluble as long as only this restricted relevancy of the entire code obtains. Even religious observance and practice presupposes an order of life that in its basic structure acknowledges the requirements of Judaism. The natural context of the Sabbath, for example, is an economic system that is itself at rest on the day. Again, only a state that recognizes them as its own official holidays can provide the truly adequate locale for the implementation of all the other religious festivals of Judaism. A great deal of the so-called conflict between traditional Judaism and twentieth-century civilization is based on a misconception. The civilization one usually has in mind is Christian. Even if the purely religious connotations of the word were to be overlooked – a hardly conceivable possibility – the factual and practical fabric of Western civilization is certainly not ideally compatible with the requirements of Jewish living.

Precisely because Judaism is itself a complete civilization, its most favorable milieu is not the lap of another civilization. What we only too often believe to be a clash between traditional concepts and the spirit of the modern age, in reality only points up the fact that the structure of a historically Christian society is not readily reconciled with the needs of Judaism. Whatever the individual Jew may think of his political status in any one country, outside the boundaries of an autonomous Jewish society Judaism is not at home. One may well be able to live in two civilizations, but no civilization can live and prosper in space which is already powerfully preempted by another. The *galut haShekhina* cannot be redeemed by political emancipation alone. Outside Eretz Yisrael only a stultified and partially stunted Judaism is possible. The separation between Zion and Torah is a spiritual catastrophe.

When Jews outside Eretz Yisrael declare that they do not form part of a diaspora, they have made a statement not only about their own political or national status but also about Judaism. They have severed Judaism from its own realm of realization. They can do so either because they no longer consider full realization of paramount importance or else because they have changed the meaning of Judaism itself. The first attitude need not detain us long: a community that believes that the *raison d'être* of its specific character is not of decisive importance is well on the way to losing its distinctiveness. Those, however, who maintain that Judaism is realizable in its entirety in any country that grants religious freedom to its citizens have implicitly adopted the tenets of the original Reform Judaism of Germany. On that basis Judaism is reduced to a credo, prayers, hours of worship, and some home customs. All this may well issue into good intentions and fine resolutions of a general humanitarian nature beyond the scant moments of contemplation and observance; the specific relevance of this type of Judaism remains limited to the private life of the Jew.

The unique significance of the Judaism of history has been that its purpose demanded application to public life as well as private life. Judaism outside Eretz Yisrael has no appropriate sphere of public application. To maintain that Judaism does not need Zion is to hold that it does not demand such application. This, however, does not mean that one rejects Jewish nationalism but rather that one limits the objective of Judaism: what historically has been an obligation upon public conscience and a standard for the public deed becomes relegated to the infinitely narrower scope of private creed and individual behavior. Such a change amounts to a transformation of essence. The individual belief that does not expect to be reflected in the organization of public life either grows otherworldly or – since this would not be in keeping with the modern mood – is watered down to a vague humanitarianism of noble intentions. What has essentially been a religious civilization is thus stripped down to a not very exciting creed whose main function it is to be a sedative at moments of trouble and visitation; the original way of life, derived from the challenge to build this world as a Kingdom of God, is turned into a gadget for securing peace of mind for the individual. It is quite possible that there are not a few Jews who may welcome such a transformation; let them not however be surprised if they will look in vain for either creative vitality or challenging relevance in their Judaism.

Such transformation of Judaism by the rules of its own logic also implies a drastic reevaluation of Jewish history. All through the ages Jews struggled, prayed, lived and died in the all-pervasive faith that the meaning of their function in history would ultimately be fulfilled in their return to Zion. Jews were prepared to die at the stake because they knew that the final reckoning was not yet; and in our own day myriads perished in the gas chambers finding their only sustenance in their "perfect faith" in the coming of the Messiah. Basically, Jewish Messianism has never been either a matter of politics or an expression of mere nationalism; it is a manifestation of the very essence of Judaism. It is the faith in the inevitable triumph of the divine purpose in history that in the course of its unfolding would cause Israel to return to the Holy Land and there, in its public life, embody Judaism. From the very beginning, Judaism contained within itself the likelihood of Exile as well as the certainty of Redemption and to be a Jew meant to accept the one and to wait for the other.

Seen in this light Jewish history does make sense: it is part of the cosmic drama of redemption. In it the massive martyrdom of Israel finds its significant role: nothing of the sorrow and the suffering was in vain, for all the time the path was being paved for the Messiah. Not a single tear was wasted, for all of it will be vindicated in his coming. Only messianic redemption can lend meaning and bring justification to Israel's martyrdom. Thus will the authenticity of the Redeemer be tested. Should he save only a contemporary generation and compel the Jewish people to write off the tragedy of two millennia in exile as a regrettable incident about which nothing more can be done, authentic Jews will know him to be another imposter. Thus, every generation looked upon itself as the guardian of all generations, seeking and acknowledging only salvation of a kind that would redeem Jewish history from the curse of a senseless martyrdom.

Let there be no mistake about it: a Jewry that believes that it is not in *galut* outside the Holy Land has broken the continuity of Jewish history; it has indeed given up Jewish Messianism; it has allowed the magnificent drama of redemption to sink to the level of meaningless misery. The prophets, the martyrs, the uncounted millions of simple people who perished believing and hoping, were all mistaken; the blood and the tears were all in vain: the Messiah has changed his destination and landed at New Amsterdam.

We see, then, how hand in hand with the transformation of the essence of Judaism, which I have discussed earlier, there goes a "reinterpretation" of Jewish history. If Judaism is only a private creed, not requiring collective implementation in the public life of history, then indeed the two thousand years of *galut* have been a deplorable episode, due to unfortunate circumstances, and the sooner it is forgotten the better for all.

At the same time, it is well to remember that we are not faced here with a genuine reevaluation either of Judaism or of Jewish history. The motivating force in this radical transformation does not spring from either religious conviction or a carefully considered new philosophy of Judaism or of history; it has its source exclusively in the political status of American Jewry. But the nature of American citizenship is something extraneous to both Judaism and the meaning of Jewish history. What Judaism is may possibly be interpreted in varied ways but the motive of interpretation must be applicable to those aspects of life with which Judaism deals. The specific quality of a man's faith in God and the discipline of living which is to follow from it can hardly be made dependent on the color of his passport. Whatever the nature of American citizenship may be, it can in no way function as a valid factor in a reinterpretation of Judaism. If it was ever seemly to believe that the redeemer would come to Zion, then the civic emancipation of the Jews in America can have no possible bearing on such a tenet of Jewish faith. It is no sign of derogation or a lack of appreciation for the United States to declare unequivocally that the essence of Judaism cannot be determined even by the finest ideals of American democracy.

The opinion that America is no *galut* is not a carefully weighed concept, but rather an understandable psychological reaction to one of the grosser aberrations of political Zionism. Having declared religion a matter of purely private concern (*Privatsache*), Zionism has attempted to sever the ideal of redemption from its original source in Judaism. Messianism has thus been reduced to the concept of political emancipation of an oppressed people. What, however, if emancipation should be accomplished outside the Jewish state? It could not be done in Europe, but what about America? Here in America, Zionism has been propagated as the answer to Jewish persecution and homelessness; a political solution to a political problem. For fifty years now the return to Zion has mainly been motivated by the negative idea of the rejection of the *galut*: the Jewish homeland was a necessity because the life of the Jewish minority in the various countries of the world was one long chain of misery. But on such a basis American Jewry could not choose Zion for itself. If *galut* is homelessness, America is no *galut* – it is an understandable conclusion. The homeless and persecuted should be helped, they better have a state of their own; American Jewry is at home in America.

It is futile to frighten the American Jew with the specter of antisemitism. He knows, of course, of its existence but, rightly or wrongly, he will not be scared. He has confidence in America and considers it his duty to stand up and fight for a fuller implementation of the ideals of freedom and equality in America. At this juncture, as a loyal citizen he cannot but follow such a course. Neither is it of much avail to attempt to embarrass him by holding before him the picture of "the invisible ghetto" in which he lives. In order to give expression to his Jewishness he does need a certain measure of separation from the general community, in his homes, Jewish centers, schools, and even Jewish neighborhoods. The invisible ghetto, once established in its ideal American form – so he may think – in fact promises the opportunity for the better integration of his Judaism into the broad pattern of American life. To badger him with accusations of insincerity in his love for Zion is truly tactless. His negative attitude to personal aliya is quite in keeping with the meager ideology of political Zionism; his emotional attachment to Zion, however, is by far stronger than that ideology by itself could ever have justified. Political Zionism cannot successfully argue against the consequences of its own logic. In the present situation, its premises – when applied to the American scene – do not point to the road to Zion. And all talk about Zionist education and cultural links with the Jewish state, about Jewish pride and self-interest, will not induce American Jewry to seek its redemption in Israel. It will support Israel; it will take genuine pride in the achievements of the Jewish state and rightly so; it will well appreciate its self-interest in the state's security and well-being; it will send visitors as well as money to Israel; it will even organize Hebrew classes; yet America will still be no *galut*. The paradoxical situation has arisen that in the phase of Zionism's triumph, its reasons for the rejection of the *galut* have conditioned hosts of good Zionists to reject the idea of *geula* in Zion for themselves.

We are reaping, then, the consequences of an insufficient Zionist ideology. Actually, on the basis of that ideology alone the rise of the Jewish state itself is hardly explicable. The Zionist analysis of Jewish homelessness was to the point; the diagnosis as well as the prognosis were correct: there was indeed need for a national home for persecuted Jews. But what right did anyone have to expect that since there was a need for it, the idea was feasible? Bearing in mind the mighty forces that were arrayed against the Zionist solution, there was little justification to believe that the goal would ever be reached. Speaking politically, even after the event, the coming into being of the Jewish state appears to be a freak occurrence; it does not rightly fit into the general pattern of power politics.

With the Jewish state something "irregular and abnormal" had entered on the world scene; nothing like it has ever happened before. Zionism will have to learn to understand its own success: the State of Israel makes sense only as a phase in the concretization of the messianic history of the Jewish people. In truth, notwithstanding the consciously conceived political ideology, the inherited messianic faith of the people has been the source of creative energy in Zionism. In the light of that faith the words of Herzl that "the Jews who wish for a State will have it" were not the empty bravado of an adventurer but an utterance in the prophetic tradition of Israel. Not the political analysis of the Jewish problem but the messianic optimism of Judaism caused him to speak in terms of certainty about the eventual successful outcome of the undertaking. And so it remained with the Zionist endeavor since the days of Herzl. It is true that in most cases Jews migrated to Palestine mainly because they were driven to do so by oppression and persecution and not because they were moved by the longing for a complete realization of Jewish concepts of living. However, while the negative idea of the rejection of the *galut* might well have been the immediate cause of actual immigration, in itself it could have hardly sufficed to provide the heroic perseverance and determination, inventiveness and creative ingenuity, without which the frightening obstacles could never have been surmounted nor the state established.

The practical requirements of temporary exigency were able to draw on the reserves of moral fortitude accumulated in the course of Jewish history. The pioneers and the leaders were the children of messianic Judaism and whatever their conscious confessions and beliefs might have been, they were sustained by its faith and inspiration. It has rightly been said of them that they were *tzaddikim* by an inner compulsion. They were able to carry the people along with them because their deeds represented a materialization of the age-old expectations of all Israel. While political Zionism believed that it could easily cut itself loose from Judaism proper, its success has been mainly due to the spiritual energies and the faith which Judaism bequeathed to the Jewish people. The messianic élan of all Israel built the State of Israel. When the state became reality Jews the world over instinctively knew that it represented a glorious vindication of the faith of Israel through the ages; with their hearts they understood that Judaism and its interpretation of history were beginning to come into their own. No wonder then that when the secular orientation of Zionist ideology was unable to cope with the awe-inspiring significance of the reestablishment of the Jewish state as an event of messianic history, the waves of exaltation that at first had engulfed the people gradually ebbed away. Zionism has let the people down. The people have not abandoned Zionism.

Unfortunately, the messianic élan of the Jewish people is itself ebbing away. And this, too, is an outcome of the European tragedy of Judaism. Prior to that catastrophe the insufficiency of political Zionism was of no serious concern. Whatever their religious or political orientation might otherwise have been, the European Jewries were that part of the Jewish people which was most deeply imbued with messianic idealism, because they were closest to the Judaism of history, the source of its origin. Whatever the consciously conceived ideology, the inherent redemptive urge of European Jewry could carry the Zionist movement toward its messianic goal. The new and young Jewries of today, however, are still lacking that intimacy with Judaism that generates the longing and, at times, even a passion for redemption. The time has therefore now come for Zionism to evaluate its own function in history for what it has truly been – an instrument of Jewish Messianism; to appreciate that its own destiny is not to be severed from the destiny of Judaism. Zionism is much more than "Auto-Emancipation"; it is the way to the complete realization of Judaism. Only so conceived may it become the personal concern of every Jew and the challenge to every Jewry. Though not to be separated from political action, *geula* is not a political concept but the aim of the messianic hunger of Israel.

On the basis of these premises the old-new ideology of *Shivat Tzion* may well be developed so that it should apply to all Jews, independently of their political status in the various countries of the world. The vital connection between Judaism, the Jewish people, and Zion must be restored. Judaism chose the people because it needed a people as the soul needs the body to enter into this world, and the people is Israel on account of Judaism; together they are in need of the land, where alone the people may become more significantly Israel by rendering Judaism more completely real. Speaking only in terms of citizenship, America may indeed be no exile for its Jews; Judaism, however, and its Jewish people are in *galut* everywhere outside Zion. The Jew who wants Judaism cannot but want Zion and by accepting Judaism he belongs to all Israel. And wherever Judaism and the Jewish people as such are in exile he too shares in their plight. The moral, spiritual, and religious destiny of every Jew, in other words that aspect of his being that alone makes him a Jew, is forever inseparable from the destiny of Zion and of all Israel.

Hence, the more intensely Jews will long for a more complete realization of Judaism for themselves, and the more they will desire that their and their children's life be invested with increased Jewish spiritual and religious content and quality, the more will they be induced to choose Zion for themselves. It is of course understood that no mass migration of American Jews to Israel is to be expected. The present quality of American Judaism is such that it may imbue only a relatively few with the urge for a fuller Jewish life of the type that can only be accomplished in Israel. However, if American Jewry is to endure at all, a genuine religious revival will have to be effected in its ranks.

As it develops, it should be possible to direct attention to Zion as the ideal realm for Judaism's full implementation. Some will then go and, as the appreciation of the need for significant living penetrates deeper and more pervasively, more and more will follow. It is true that thus far purely idealistic motives hardly ever prevailed upon large numbers to settle in Eretz Yisrael. Today, the situation is unique in that a novel and potentially powerful factor must be reckoned with: the State of Israel is a reality. As the vital link between Judaism and Zion is restored and Israel rises once again in the eyes of the Jewish people to its true dignity as the incipient phase in the messianic fruition of Jewish history, the prospect of living in Eretz Yisrael will capture the imagination of many Jews. And as, in time, the Jewish state itself achieves greater consolidation so that the measure of material sacrifice involved in aliya is considerably reduced, there is reason to hope that thousands of Jews may be prepared to leave annually from America for settlement in Israel. It is of hardly less importance that a Jewry that interprets Judaism as incomplete without Zion, and views the messianic urge of Jewish history as moving toward its satisfaction in the Holy Land, will maintain a dynamic relationship of personal concern, love, and responsibility for Eretz Yisrael.

The loyalty of the American Jew as a citizen is neither involved in such a position nor is it in any way affected by it. The duties and obligations of citizenship remain untouched; they must not be interfered with by any form of allegiance to any other state. But the life of a human being is not completely circumscribed by citizenship alone; it is only partially embraced by forms of political organization. The loyalty of citizenship is not the only one incumbent upon a man. A Jew who leaves America for Israel in search of a more complete Judaism does not reject America but chooses Zion; he does not find fault with America but seeks to meet religious and spiritual needs of his being whose satisfaction is certainly outside the scope and the objectives of American citizenship.

Of course "Israel" does not exist only on the messianic level of history; it is a very real political organization that is involved in the international frame of power politics. To anticipate however a genuine conflict of loyalties as a result of American Jewry's vital interest in Israel is in itself more the sign of an overanxious *galut* mentality than the convincing mark of a Jewry fully emancipated in a free democracy. That the State of Israel enjoys its due chance to exist and prosper is indeed the ardent desire of all Jews and one must assume that they share this wish with all fair-minded people the world over. But especially for American Jews it should be inconceivable that such a requirement of international justice and decency could at any time be contrary to the interest of the American people; to think otherwise of America would indeed be an insult to the moral dignity of a great people and its finest traditions. The nervous sensitiveness of some American Jews to the bogey of a conflict of loyalties is not exactly a compliment to America, but there is no need to charge it to one or the other of the imperfections of American democracy; it is a melancholy sign that even though America is no *galut* for its citizens, there are Jews in America who have not yet acquired the civic courage and the mature sense of responsibility that should go with citizenship in a truly free democracy.

Possibly, things could be made easier if one could "simplify" both Judaism and Jewish peoplehood, if one could separate the one from the other; especially, if one could sever American Judaism from the rest of Israel and from Jewish history. But one cannot do it and preserve either Judaism or the people. It is understandable that every now and then there will be Jews who hope to simplify matters by trying to "normalize" themselves. Political Zionism has attempted to do it by separating nationhood from Judaism, declaring Jews to be a nation like any other. Actually, by the establishment of the Jewish state Jews have not become more "normal" but less so. And unless Zionism is prepared to write off the overwhelming majority of the Jewish people living outside "Israel," its process of simplification has dismally failed. At all times there have also been those who follow the opposite course. According to them, Judaism is a religion like any other and is independent of any specific country or nationality. What is left does indeed drastically simplify everything, for the result is extinction by assimilation. Jews will therefore better give up their hankering after "normalcy"; the moment they become "normal" they cease to be Jews. Not to fit into generally accepted modes of classification may indeed at times bring complications in its wake, but to trim one's personality so as to fit into them at all cost is much worse; it means dissolution. If Jews do wish to survive, let them accept the consequences of their distinctiveness. American Jews in particular may do well to recall these words of George Santayana: "Special circumstances had given us hereditary points of attachment in opposite quarters, moral and geographical; and now... I may say that we proved remarkably staunch in our complex allegiances, combining them as well as logic allowed, without at heart ever disowning anything."

The Sounds of the Modern Jewish Neighborhood

One late summer afternoon as I was walking through a Jewish neighborhood, my attention was caught by an interesting scene. A number of people were sitting in two groups on the porch of a middle-class home. One group was formed by the patriarchal figure of an old Jew. He was a man rich in years, obviously approaching the close of his earthly pilgrimage. His head was covered with the traditional "yarmulka" and his face, adorned with a long, graying beard. He was sitting in an armchair deeply engrossed in what was undoubtedly a "*sefer*" from the traditional literature of Judaism.

At some little distance from the old man was sitting the other group. They were younger people apparently of the same family – possibly children of the old Jew, or, perhaps, his grandchildren. They were silent also but absorbed in the reading of newspapers that were scattered around and about them in almost numberless sheets.

The old man did look like a complete group all by himself. Here were two *worlds* on that porch: the one of "Zaide" and the other of "Zaide's" children; two worlds alike and side by side, but one could sense the gulf – unbridgeable – that separated the one from the other. There were a father and his children, so close to each other in space and yet far removed from each other in communication.

There was silence on the porch and somehow one realized that it meant: we have nothing to say to each other. However, there was something else too about that silence. Silence could easily be made into a most rewarding subject of study. There are almost as many different kinds of silences as there are noises. There is, for example, the silence of an empty apartment. It "sounds" differently from the silence of an apartment that is a *home*, in which people live and which is silent because, after a day's work and play, parents and children have retired and the house is at rest.

Two people may be silent because they have nothing to say to each other; but there may also be silence of an entirely different quality between two people who love each other – who do not speak because they understand each other without words. There is a silence of anger, the "icy silence," and there is also a kindly and encouraging one that is a balm to the heart. The two groups on the veranda were separated from each other even by nature of their silences. For the truth was – and it was probably the most striking feature of the scene which I happened to observe – that there were two different silences there: the one surrounding the father reading the *sefer*, the other around the children with their newspapers.

The silence about the old man had a dignity of its own; it meant thinking and contemplation, it had a fragrance like that of old wine. It was a most eloquent silence, for if one listened carefully one could hear it say: There is so much to think about, so much one ought to endeavor to understand. And it is good to sit and think and to ponder on what others before us, saints, prophets, and teachers thought and taught... and now and then to put the good book down for a while and to think our own thoughts and dream our own dreams, stimulated by the book.

The old man's silence was saying all this and much more, but his children did not hear it. They were far away roving restlessly over endless sheets of black print. They were barricaded behind their own silence. And what a different silence it was. It revealed to the observer that the children had just finished their evening meal and it was too early yet either for their favorite TV program or for the show they were planning to see that night. What could one do at such a moment between work and entertainment? To converse? To think? Perhaps to read a book? About what?... The children's silence spoke of boredom and mental exhaustion.

The newspapers that the younger group read were thrown away the next morning; the book in the hands of the old man was read and treasured by many generations in the past. The old man will put the book away for tomorrow and the next day and for the day after that. But one day "Zaide" will no longer be sitting on the porch. What will then happen to the book? Will there be only one silence left – the silence of irrelevance, grazing over the very latest nickel-wisdom of a soon-forgotten evening paper?

Philosophical and Theological Dimensions in *Galut**

You are all aware of the theme of this convention, "*Am VeEmuna: Le'an?* (People and Faith, Whither?)"

I believe that the theme, in a sense, reflects an embarrassment of the modern Jew. Two or three generations ago, such a theme would have made no sense, for there was nothing more natural for a Jew than to be a Jew. And as far as the relationship between *Am* and *Emuna* was concerned, the statement of Saadia Gaon that we are a people *bizkhut hatora,* because of the Torah, was so self-evident that it was not necessary to raise it into full consciousness.

And as to "*Le'an?*" – everybody knew: we lived in the *galut* temporarily and we were all the time on our way to Eretz Yisrael. Today we are struggling for self-understanding. And there exists a plethora of

* Rabbi Berkovits delivered this address before the Reform Movement's Central Conference of American Rabbis in June 1981.

interpretations of what it is to be Jewish: what it means to live the life of a Jew, what Judaism is, what the goals are we ought to pursue.

In my discussion I intend to start with an analysis of two positions which are radically opposed to each other and are yet very closely related to each other. The one is expressed in a rather well-known short story by Haim Hazaz, an Israeli writer, titled "HaDerasha" (The Homily). It has very little to do with the sermons that are preached in Reform or Conservative or Orthodox synagogues. And the other interpretation emerges from the philosophy of Franz Rosenzweig.

Now, according to "HaDerasha," the Jews in the *galut* were not a people. Their whole life was imposed upon them; their history was made for them by others, but now – as a result of Zionism that returned them to Eretz Yisrael – this group of people, held together until now by a common misery, has become a nation, taking its own destiny in its own hands, creating its own history.

At the radically opposite end, we find the interpretation of Franz Rosenzweig. According to him, "*Ḥayei olam nata betokheinu*," God has planted eternal life into our midst as a result of His revelation of the Torah to us, to the Jewish people. But what is eternal life? Eternal life in this world, not *la'olam haba*; eternal life down here. According to Franz Rosenzweig, it is life above change; life without the vitality inherent in change. It is the eternal now – above time, above history. The Jewish people, says Rosenzweig, does not really belong to the world of time and development; it has already reached the *eschaton*; it is at the *omega* of the road, having found fulfillment and redemption, and now it is waiting for the others to catch up with it. And of necessity – because of that – it is a people without a home, without a homeland. The Holy Land has a function not to allow this people to take root in any one country, and the holy language (which is only the language of prayer) means that in no language can this people find its spiritual home.

Now it is remarkable how close these two interpretations are to each other, in spite of the fact that they are apparently radically opposed to each other. For both of them see the same phenomena before them, in front of them. Both of them see passivity, lifelessness, lack of vitality, no history. Rosenzweig spiritualizes all of this: Passivity, lack of change, holiness means being above time; holiness means to live the life of lifelessness. Of course, the secular author of "HaDerasha" could not spiritualize in this sense. What he saw was an impossible situation: only passivity, only lack of history, no change, no development.

I believe that both of them are wrong. The author of "HaDerasha" is wrong in interpreting the phenomena before him, and Franz Rosenzweig is wrong in his understanding of Judaism as *ḥayei olam,* that is, the life of lifeless holiness.

As to the facts – it's just not true that Jewish life in the *galut* was a life of passivity. On the contrary, Jewish life in the *galut* was a life of highest activity. It is not true that in the *galut* history was made for the Jew. The truth is that the Jew in the *galut,* for many centuries, right up to the days of Nazism, was always standing before a choice. He could always embrace the religion of the majority culture around him and thus escape persecution and oppression. The Jew made his choice in inner freedom, knowing well the bitter price he would have to pay for it.

If Ahad Ha'am once described the position of the assimilated, post-emancipation Jew as living in *avdut betokh ḥeirut,* in slavery in the midst of freedom – one might say that for many centuries the Jew of the *galut* lived in *ḥeirut betokh avdut,* in inner freedom in spite of slavery.

Galut Jewry also possessed a self-sustaining and self-creating culture and civilization: its own system of values, its own beliefs by which it lived and which it applied consistently to every situation in which it found itself. This so-called "passive Jewry" had a system of general education obligatory for all levels of society already in talmudic times, when none of the modern nations even had an idea what was meant by general education.

This "passive Jewry" without history had a system of communal welfare sustained by its own resources – the *tamḥui* in talmudic times, the *hekdesh* in the ghettos – caring for the poor and the sick.

This Jewry of the *galut* sustained all through the ages a high measure of self-governing autonomy. Not only in those days when such autonomy was granted to the Jewish communities by the civil and political powers under which they lived, but even after that. Even when this official authorization had not been granted, Jewish communities administered their own affairs on the basis of an internal autonomy, by a freely accepted discipline – the discipline of the halakha.

I remember myself still: in our communities in Eastern Europe, no self-respecting Jew would go to a civil court in case of litigation. He submitted to a *beit din*. And all this was accomplished without a police force, without the power of a state, without an army.

Galut Jewry created great literatures – the Talmud in Babylon and in Eretz Yisrael; midrashim, codes, *piyutim*, philosophical works. And in all the countries where they absorbed the alien language of the majority culture, soon they turned this alien language into their own means of expression – expressing their own life experience by specific idiomatic phraseology, by specific syntax; expressing in it their own wisdom, their own humor; creating in it literature and poetry. Think only of Yiddish; modern Hebrew literature has yet a long way to go in order to reach the creative quality of Yiddish literature and Yiddish poetry. Some of the greatest poetry and some of the greatest modern Hebrew poets, Tchernichovsky, Bialik, Agnon – to mention only a few – were of *galut* vintage.

We have been one people in the *galut* in a much more intimate sense than any other nation on this earth has ever been one people.

Thus far as to the facts. Theologically, Rosenzweig was altogether wrong in maintaining that the eternal life of God's revelation raised us above the flow of time and history. On the contrary: it is possible to affirm that among all civilizations, Judaism was the first one that conceived of history as a process, as a development toward a goal, toward a fulfillment of universal values on this earth. Striving for the realization of those values is the messianic ideal. Just think of the concept of *Aḥarit HaYamim*, the End of Days, of the continual reference to the phrase *Vehaya bayom hahu*, "And it will be on that day." It all speaks of change, of development, of process, of a goal to come.

Neither is it correct to say that holiness in Judaism is a life of lifelessness. On the contrary. It's enough to think of a few verses in *Parashat Kedoshim*: "*Kedoshim tihyu ki kadosh Ani Adonai Eloheikhem*, Be holy, for I am holy; I, the Lord your God." What follows? Laws which mean involvement in life, social legislation. Or think of the phrase "*Letaken olam bemalkhut Shadai*," which sums up Jewish responsibility as meaning to establish this world as a Kingdom of God.

It would seem to me that the problem here arises from the fact that we have been accustomed to interpret ourselves in categories which are alien to our existence, alien to our ideals, alien to our history, and which are valid in the non-Jewish world.

Indeed, there, in this non-Jewish world, a people without a land of their own, without a language for the mundane use of everyday life, without a state, without a government, without police, without army – is not a nation. There – homeland, material power, political independence, or striving for political independence, are the preconditions for national history and for national existence. If one applies these categories to the Jewish people in the *galut*, then indeed we are not a people; we have no history. (And I'm not terribly upset about it.) Then indeed our existence is mere passivity, or – if you are a mystically inclined theologian – a life of holy lifelessness, above time and history.

I'm coming to the second part of your convention; I come to the concept of *emuna*. I believe that the time has come for us to have the courage to know ourselves, to recognize ourselves, to look at ourselves not with alien categories, but with the categories that derive from the very essence of our historic existence; and to have the courage, as a result of self-knowledge, to accept the truth that we are not just another people, but a *different* people. Of course, we are a people. However, if you look upon what constitutes peoplehood in the rest of the world as a norm, we have to confess that we are not a normal people.

Thank God that we are not normal people! What puzzles us and what puzzles others is the fact that we are *goy eḥad ba'olam*. A nation that lives, preserves its identity, sustains its own culture and civilization, chooses to live by its own values and beliefs in continuous confrontation, and does it for millennia in a condition of homelessness and material powerlessness – is indeed one nation, a unique people on this earth.

What of its history? It certainly is not made of the same substance of which the history of other nations is made. Through its entire history in the *galut* it was lacking all those material resources without which no nation has been able to exist. But Israel lived by a different strength. In one of my books I distinguish between "power history" and "faith history." Today we'd like to change the term "faith history" to "messianic history."

I am fully aware of the fact that, unfortunately, here in Israel the very word "messianism" has become a dirty word, almost as dirty as "religious Judaism," maybe even more dirty. Yes, ours has been messianic history, and by that I don't mean only that we have faith in the coming of the Messiah (a faith that certainly had its psychological significance and its psychological power to save us from despair). I'm speaking of the reality of history, of the facts of our history; and I call the reality of our history, the facts of our history, "messianic history." I mean by it, I understand by it – the reality of Jewish existence through the ages which was different from the realities of the existence of other nations, and by means that were different from means by which they existed. I mean by "messianic history," the working reality of the Jewish commitment, the working reality through history of the covenantal relationship between the Jew and God.

I call it "messianic" because it is an intrinsic part of the process that the messianic idea envisages as leading ultimately – be it even by a tortuous path – to universal fulfillment and redemption.

The functioning of the Jewish commitment (in spite of everything that has been done through history to rub it off the face of the earth) – its ever-recovering force, its ever-renewing creative power – proves that that process of messianic fulfillment toward which history leads is indeed at work. Jewish history is, therefore, messianic history. And it alone explains Jewish survival.

My "friend" Toynbee (strangely enough, he once wrote in his work "Reconsideration" that the only one of his critics that understood him was Eliezer Berkovits; but it didn't help him very much) – Toynbee interprets the existence, the survival of the Jewish people as a fossil. And I think this interpretation is characteristic of all extant philosophies of history. Toynbee had a grandiose plan for world history according to which civilizations rise, decline, and fall. There was one nation, one people, that caused him trouble, became a nuisance – the Jews. They didn't fit into his grandiose plan. He had an ingenious idea: the Jews – never mind, they don't exist, they are a fossil. It is almost true of all generally accepted philosophies of history. We don't fit in there; we are intruders. We are living in a different historic dimension; a historic dimension that transcends power history; we are intruders. A long time ago, in the Midrash, the Rabbis already explained the significance of the name Avraham Avinu: "*Lama nikra shemo Avraham HaIvri? Kol ha'olam kulo me'ever eḥad, vehu me'ever eḥad*" – the whole world is on one side, and Avraham Avinu is on the other side (Genesis Rabba 42:8).

The significance of this statement, my friends, is valid to this day. Of course, not all non-Jews that are puzzled by us are as "kind" to us as Toynbee was. Since they are unable to fit us into the world structure which they created for themselves, they, in a way (without being aware of it, indirectly) acknowledge the transcending significance of our presence, or our endurance, of our reality in world history, by distorting and falsifying that reality. In the Middle Ages, they looked upon us as being in league with the devil. In this more enlightened, modern age we are often considered as some kind of underground, international conspiracy – a threat to the world.

I had some experience with Nazism. I saw them come to power and I lived under them, and often I had to face the Gestapo itself eye to eye. Perhaps the most remarkable aspect of the Nazi hatred of the Jew was the fear of the Jewish people by which it was fed.

When they said, "The Jews are our misfortune," they really believed it. Remarkable! At one time they were the greatest military power on earth, and yet they were afraid somehow of the Jewish influence. They were afraid. And rightly so!...

Not altogether dissimilar is the relationship of Soviet Communism to the continued existence of the Jewish people. Nikolai Berdyaev, one of the outstanding Russian existentialists, writes in one of his books that he originally accepted Marxist materialism, dialectic materialism, but when he became acquainted with the history of the Jewish people, he was forced to give it up, because he saw from the history of the Jewish people that dialectical materialism cannot be right. And to this day, the dogmatists in the Kremlin seem to realize that somehow the continued existence of the Jewish people, its effective functioning as a preserver and renewer of its own culture and civilization, is an intellectual as well as moral challenge to Marxist materialism.

Le'an, my friends? I believe that self-understanding, the courage of self-understanding, is especially vital for us in this age of the *Shoah.* We usually speak of the six million Jews as if they had been six million individual human beings. But they were not only individual Jews; they were the very core of Jewish peoplehood. They were communities that existed for many centuries – with schools, *batei midrash, yeshivot,* cultural institutions, *minhagim* that formed Jewish character imperceptibly, by the accumulated Jewish experience, memories, wisdom of many generations.

We were not only reduced in numbers, we have become a ruined people. And we have to rebuild. Before anything else, we have to be ourselves; we have to return to ourselves. We must beware of becoming a normal people. It seems to me that one of the problems of Jewish life in Israel is the drive to become a normal people. Especially the young generation believes that Zionism means a process of normalization.

The moment we become a normal people we shall cease to be Jews; we shall cease to be a Jewish people. I am fully aware of the fact that there are many people who think that might not be so bad. But I cannot think of anything more unworthy of the magnitude, of the significance of the reestablishment of the State of Israel than now to indulge in a drive for normalcy.

That after two thousand years of *galut* – such a *galut* – there still was in existence a Jewish people that was able to establish itself in the homeland of its fathers, that, "flying into the face of all history," always maintained that one day it will come back – that this happened is one of the greatest, most abnormal things that ever happened in the history of mankind. And Ben-Gurion was right when, at the time of the establishment of the state, he said, "This is the greatest miracle in history."

And now to misuse it, as the beginning of a process of normalization to become normal *kekhol haamim,* a normal nation – this is a defeat. The fruits of the normalization process in Israel are rather bitter. It has produced a generation that does not know *me'ayin bata,* from where it came, and does not know *le'an ata holekh,* where it is headed. It has caused some of the best youth in Israel to become uncertain of our moral right to this country. And because of that, uncertainty eats away at the roots of idealism. How is this country to be maintained and continue to be built without idealism?

A disturbingly large section of the Israeli population understands the process of becoming a normal people as the vulgar imitation of some of the ugliest features of American materialism. That normalization does not work is shown by the tragically high rate of *yerida*, departure, from Israel – a return to the fleshpots of modern decadence.

Furthermore, recasting us into a normal mold of nationhood would mean using the ruins of our people in order to create a new nation. Personally, I'm not interested in creating a new nation; and I believe the majority of the Jews in the world are not interested in using the remnants of the Jewish people for the purpose of creating a new nation. This is one of the main reasons why the decrease in aliya has become proportionate to the increase in *yerida* from Israel. The return to the land may prove to be meaningless without a return to ourselves.

What about the Jewish people in the *Tefutzot*, living beyond the borders of Israel? I believe it's generally understood that notwithstanding all the problems of life in Israel, this is the place for the essential aspects of rebuilding a ruined people. And since what is happening and being done here will ultimately determine – whether we like it or not – the destiny of our people all over the world, it is vital that the Diaspora involves itself *personally* (and not only by checks), actively, in the continued rebuilding of *Am Yisrael biMedinat Yisrael*, the Jewish people in the State of Israel. It is vital that in the Diaspora we develop a Judaism that has a quality that will present the vital section of Jewish youth in America with aliya as a demanding and challenging option.

I'm not asking that the *Tefutzot* become completely Israel-oriented. I should like to see the *Tefutzot* become Judaism-oriented – not for the sake of Israel, but for the sake of the survival of Judaism in a significant manner all over the world.

We have to rediscover the spiritual strength, the spiritual resources of Judaism – no matter what our ideologies may be. We have to strive to eliminate Jewish ignorance. We have to have the courage to embrace our Jewish destiny – our historic Jewish reality – and restore Judaism to a way of daily life, so that it will cease to be an occasion for celebrations and observances, cease to be just another religion.

Our situation in the world is fundamentally different from the times in which all the extant ideologies were formulated. And because of this fundamental difference, I believe that all our ideologies require review and revision – Reform, Conservative, and Orthodox.

The realization of this need for review and revision may help us bring down the walls that divide us. Each one, in accordance with his own conscience, should meet the challenges of our days, and meet them as *one* people.

Permit me to conclude by paraphrasing some words which I had the pleasure of sending to a congregation that was honoring a very dear friend of mine who is a distinguished member of your organization. "Although we find ourselves in different camps, let those camps not be opposing ones. Along different paths let us walk together, work as one people, for the rebuilding of our people from the ruins of this tragic age. True to our conscience, in our unity we shall yet discover that *Netzaḥ Yisrael lo yeshaker,* Israel's Eternal God will not betray us."

Section 3

Return

God and National Existence

In our plan for closing the gap between Torah and Life an all-important part must be assigned to the return of the Jewish nation to the Holy Land. A Jewish Eretz Yisrael is the only place where the great partnership between Torah and Life can be restored, without which Judaism is doomed. It is necessary now to define with some precision the role that is to be allotted to Jewish national existence within the system of Judaism.

We have dealt with modern Jewish nationalism in a previous chapter.[1] But national existence is not nationalism; national existence is a fact, nationalism is a conception. National existence is a kind of life, nationalism a manifestation of willpower. The national unit, insofar as it is an aggregate of living beings, is part of a greater unit; it is a biological entity that subserves the purpose of the whole. Nationalism, the unity of conscious aims, converts this small section of mankind, the national aggregate, into a self-contained unit, thus elevating the part to the dignity of a whole – even of the whole. But whoever elevates the section

1. Eliezer Berkovits, *Towards Historic Judaism* (Oxford: The East and West Library, 1943), 37–51.

into the whole does so at the cost of other sections that are constituents of the legitimate whole.

Whereas the national unit, as a biological entity, is beyond good or evil, the substitution of the nationalistic aspirations for what may be called the humanistic, as if the nation were the be-all and end-all of things, belongs to the worst category of idolatry. It implies the sanctification of the selfish ambitions and desires of the national unit, and sets up the interests of the nation as the only standard of action. A nationalism carried to extremes will always usurp the Throne of God by placing on it the national ideal. Of course, nationalism need not always be extremist, need not always be carried to its logical conclusions, may not always have the courage to do so, and may often be lacking the power to throw down the challenge to the rest of the world. But where nationalism is carried to the point where the interests of the nation are regarded as the supreme authority, the result is that all the individual egotisms are bundled together into one national egotism, which thus becomes the most monstrous idol mankind has worshipped in all its aberrations. It is hardly possible to imagine a more dangerous crime than such nationalism, for no other has brought so much robbery, suffering, bloodshed, and bestiality into the world; and all that clad in the mantle of idealism and heroism.

It cannot be doubted for a single moment that in the system of Judaism there is no place for such nationalism. The acknowledgment of God as the supreme authority, carries with it the recognition of the religious and ethical values based upon monotheism as the only standards for human action and behavior, and overrides all other ends. You either serve God or Baal; monotheism does not allow compromise.

A Jewish nationalism of this kind would be a contradiction in terms. If it were Jewish it could not be nationalist, if nationalist it could never be Jewish. Naturally enough, individual Jews may be nationalists of this type. There is no end to the possibilities of Jewish failures, especially in the midst of a world gone mad with successful nationalistic idolatry. As in biblical times so today, we Jews are only too ready to imitate the idolatries of the world around us, for as then so today, they appeal most strongly to the weaknesses of human nature. But the repudiation of such nationalism does not mean the renunciation of a Jewish national existence. The Jewish national unit is an undeniable historic fact. We are a living nation, and as with everything living we have in us the natural desire to live. For no just or logical reason can this right to live be denied us. There are certain minimum necessities of national existence, and it is imperative that these at least should be satisfied. But let us make up our mind once and for all, that though we want to live it must not be at *any* price. (Judaism, but for a few individual aberrations, has remained true for thousands of years of Jewish history to this great principle.) A Jewish national policy must not be determined by Jewish national interest alone. Whatever Jewish national policy may be, it is still accountable to the moral code, based upon Jewish monotheism. This may not always be the most immediately successful way of achieving our aims. But when was easy success an all-important motive in our history? Let us rather be unsuccessful than unfaithful. The essence of the Jewish national cause is justice; and justice is a formidable enough weapon in a world in which, we believe, it is bound to triumph in the end. And we Jews shall live to see the fulfillment of that persistent Jewish dream.

National existence and Judaism are more closely related than we have so far indicated. The national unit is an essential part of the system of Judaism. This is often deeply felt by Jews but seldom clearly understood. Judaism is often called a national religion. There exists, indeed, an intimate connection between Nation and what is usually called Religion. We have the Jewish festivals, which though religious in character are commemorations of important national events. We have the many religious regulations which seem to be intended to safeguard and preserve racial purity and national cohesion. There are many laws of the Torah applicable only within the nation. There is a whole land policy of a religious nature which is applicable only in Eretz Yisrael. The Torah offers us a national constitution based on religious principles. It is, indeed, correct to assert that no Judaism is possible without Jewish national existence.

On the other hand, however, there exists another and broader conception of Judaism, very prominent in the prophets, the great idea of a universal religion, of a world in which all are worshipping the One

God, who chooses His priests from among *all* the nations. This universalism of the prophets can hardly find a proper place in a national religion; it breaks through the national framework. There is, of course, the idea, very eagerly put forward by non-Jewish Bible critics especially, of a great religious development in Israel from its primitive belief in a tribal deity to a later universalism. These ingenious hypotheses are for us completely irrelevant. Judaism is not a relic of the past that has to be dug out from biblical allusions or antiquarian discoveries. Here we are, a whole nation, the children of the prophets, representing *living Judaism*; not only with the memory of a tribal deity obliterated, but with fundamental principles originally promulgated to counter any such idolatrous conceptions.

Whatever the early religious ideas of the Semitic tribes, our Judaism commenced with a pure monotheism, God the Creator of the Universe, the Father of all nations and all men. What does it prove if Jews often relapsed into the pre-monotheistic ways, if they were not always able to distinguish clearly between the tribal creeds that flourished around them and the idea of the One God? Jewish failures are no representation of Judaism. Universalism is at the root of Judaism and was contained in it from its very beginning. Judaism stands or falls with it. Universalism is not a new development within Judaism, only a new conscious realization by Jews of its full meaning.

For this reason all talk about a Jewish "national religion," is not only misrepresentation but falsification. The term "national religion," so very popular these days even among Jews, is only the old tribal deity in other words. It is idolatrous. The idea of God is anational; monotheism does not fit the national frame. In its very essence monotheism is universalistic. And yet, it remains a fact that this universalistic Judaism is inseparably attached to Jewish national existence. This is, indeed, a baffling paradox. It is natural that individual Jews should lay stress either on the universalistic or the national features of historic conceptions according to temperament and religious or political inclinations. Thus, in the camp of the Jewish national movement Judaism became the national religion, whereas liberal assimilationism converted it into a vague, noncommittal, theoretical universalism, divested of its historic national basis. It is time to free ourselves from such one-sided theologies and sincerely try to face the whole problem presented by the peculiar combination of national existence and a universalism that cannot recognize national barriers.

In order to understand this combination, one must bear in mind that the term "religion" as normally understood among Western peoples is not applicable to Judaism. In fact, in Hebrew there exists no word that expresses what is usually meant by that term. The nearest biblical expressions to what is commonly meant by "religion" are "*Daat Hashem*" or "*Derekh Hashem*" (the Knowledge of God, or the Way of God). Judaism is not a system of creeds and dogmas; it is not concentration on "divine worship" at certain places and certain times, nor is it mystical intercourse of the few selected ones with God; it is intended to be Knowledge and Teaching, it is a Way.

Knowledge of God means that the whole system possesses only one fundamental belief, the belief in a personal God. Everything else is knowledge, i.e., it is either logically derived from the basic idea of the personal God, or it is revealed in history. (The thirteen "*Ikkarim*"[2] [Dogmas] of Maimonides are no credo; they represent a theological disputation with other religious systems.) And the Way of God is the way that men should walk as a logical outcome of their belief in God. Although it is impossible to define it in a few words, it probably comes nearest to the truth to say that Judaism is no "religion" but a Way of Living based upon the belief in a personal God.

That the idea of a personal God should lead to the Way of Living is perfectly logical. For a personal God means a personally ever-present God; a God continually looking on, continually looking at you. It means that all life is always and everywhere life in the presence of God. The conception of life given by God and to be lived in the perennial presence of God must inescapably lead to a definite way of living. For God is looking on to see, and in giving us life He has given us the chance to show what we are. God's eyes, watching us, render life always and everywhere the God-given testing ground of men. Wherever we are,

2. Not to be confused with the *Ani Maamin*, which, though based on Maimonides, was formulated later, undoubtedly under the influence of the importance of the credo in Christianity.

whatever we do, we are being tested and watched. This is the situation with which man is confronted as long as he lives. The conception of life as the inescapable testing ground of man demands a Way of Living that embraces the whole of life, every branch of it, every moment of it; a way that must be signalized by an awareness of the eternal Divine Presence and by the endeavor of man to stand that test always and everywhere without relaxing for one moment.

This is not the place to develop this thought and to show in detail how Judaism tried to realize the consequences of its basic belief in a personal God, Creator of the Universe. Enough to say that Jewish monotheism aims at forcing the *whole* of life into a clean-cut direction which will uplift it and give it meaning.

The whole of life is primarily the whole of one's personal life. But the individual life is never a whole, it is inextricably interwoven with innumerable other individual lives. To be able to master one's own life as a whole, one must make common cause with all the other individual lives to which one's own life is related, socially, economically, politically, in short with all the many relations that matter in life. Life is always a whole bundle of life. That is why the Way of Living can never be the task of the individual. One can worship God individually, one can have faith individually, but one cannot succeed as an individual in molding the whole of life, even so far as one alone is concerned. For the life of the individual is always part of a larger life, and only where this larger life can be, so to speak, mobilized is the Way of Living to be realized. The power to do this, so essential for the realization of Judaism, is never possessed by the individual, it always belongs to the whole life-circle of which he is only a constituent part. Only a whole life-unit or circle can ever be independent enough to be able to exercise the controlling power necessary to shape living reality in accordance with the monotheistic conception of God.

Judaism cannot be realized by the individual. It must be grounded on an autonomous life unit, which, of course, is no quantitative but a qualitative term. The number of those confessing Judaism is not decisive; even millions of individual adherents, spread all over the world, do not make the realization of Judaism possible. They all would belong to diverse social and economic groups following entirely different directions from the one demanded by Jewish realization. They all could believe in Judaism but not live it. The autonomous life-unit is no gathering of individual believers; it is an organic group with command over its own social, economic, cultural, and political relations. Theoretically it is conceivable that if a sufficient number of adherents extricated themselves from their former surroundings, and came together in some unoccupied place, they could start the realization of their ideals; in that case they would soon find themselves changing into an organic group.

Whether or not it was something similar that actually happened at the beginning of Jewish history when Abraham left his father's house and native land, as related in the Bible, is not important in this connection. The only thing of real importance is the fact that the first Jew had to be the father of a nation, for the organic group that is the necessary basis of the realization of the Way of Living always appears in human history as a biological unit, the tribe, the nation, etc. That is why Abraham did not establish a school or a church; he had to stand at the head of a national unit. This does not mean that the national unit is the frame enclosing Judaism; it has nothing to do with national religion. The organic tribal or national group is the smallest possible unit within which monotheism can be realized. The intimate relationship between Jewish national existence and universalistic Judaism is conditioned by the fact that the organic group is the unit of realization. Universalistic monotheism is not individualistic, it is collectivistic; it cannot be realized by individual believers, but only by organic groups of believers.

The consequences of such a conception of Judaism are, I think, quite clear. It repudiates the universalism of assimilationist liberal Jewry. This Jewry trying to dispense with national existence in the name of the universalism of the prophets is actually changing the essence of Judaism. Such Jews can dispense with the national unit only because they discard the most important feature of Judaism, the Way of Living. Judaism is no longer a way, it becomes a church, it ceases to be Judaism.

But neither, on the other hand, does the collectivistic conception of Jewish universalism allow for the ordinary forms of nationalism.

The Jewish national unit is an instrument serving a higher purpose that in its very essence is anational. But, in order to be an effective working instrument, the national unit must control its own life. This means that for Jews to live dispersed all over the world in the midst of strange surroundings, necessarily moving to the rhythm of a life different from that of the Jewish national unit, is an unnatural form of "Judaistic" existence. *Galut* may at times be a historic necessity, it may produce its own great values, but it must always be looked upon as a period of transition, something temporary, not only from the national point of view but also from that of the realization of Judaism. Complete realization is an impossibility in the *galut*.

Many important precepts of the Torah have to be put into cold storage, as it were, for the duration of the *galut*, simply because Jews lack the concrete basis to which to apply them. The whole system of Jewish jurisprudence, for instance, has been shelved, for naturally enough in the *galut* there exists only *dina d'malkhuta*, the law of the state in which Jews happen to live. All the social and economic regulations relating to the possession of national land are *hilkh'ta l'meshiḥa*, the law for the messianic age, as long as Jews live in exile. Even where realization is possible, it is only partial and stunted. For instance, the laws of the *Even HaEzer* section of the *Shulḥan Arukh*, which in normal times constituted the law for an important part of Jewish family and social life, have been more and more reduced in the *galut* to a mere religious ceremonial. The "legality" of that sphere of Jewish life rests on the respective marriage and divorce laws of the state in which Jews happen to live. What has remained of the talmudic order Nashim in actual practice is a mere shadow of the original. This is also true of many other parts of Judaism in the *galut*. It is natural that the Sabbath as envisaged in a Jewish community determining its own social and economic life in accordance with its own conception of a Day of Rest is entirely different from a Sabbath observed in the midst of a society which takes its rest in its own manner on its own Sunday.

In respect of every Jewish activity in the *galut* we are confronted with the fact that Judaism, being a Way of Living, can only be realized to a limited extent in the midst of surroundings over which Jews have no decisive influence. *Galut* Judaism is bound to remain a shadow Judaism. Jews have always made the greatest sacrifices to maintain their Judaism, to keep it alive in spite of the *galut*. It is an awe-inspiring story of faith and courage and hope, this determination of Jews to realize their Judaism in the midst of antagonistic forces and in defiance of them, that heroic determination of millions and millions of *galut* Jews not to bow to these alien forces, not to acknowledge them, and to go on living as if they did not exist. But the very fact that Judaism in *galut* has become identified with sacrifice testifies only too painfully to the anomaly of *galut* existence. Judaism is sacrificed when it has to be realized by Jews whose everyday life is determined by an alien environment. Originally it was the harmony in the existence of a nation which produced the rhythm of its own life. For us Jews monotheistic universalism requires a Jewish national unit where the potentialities of Judaism are fully realizable, i.e., a Jewish nation master in its own home. Judaism may be able to survive for yet a long time in the *galut*, but only in the Jewish National Home can it be naturally and completely realized. The national unit is the instrument, the National Home the place of realization.

Let us not forget too for a single moment that we cannot start anew today: we can but continue. For that reason the place of the Jewish National Home is historically given. There is only one Zion and only one Jerusalem, one Holy Land, one Eretz Yisrael.

As the purpose of the Jewish national unit is primarily to serve monotheistic universalism, it cannot cut itself off from the rest of the world. It must always remain conscious of the fact that monotheism is meant for the whole of mankind, and recognizes no frontiers as barriers between man and man. The universalistic application of the idea of a personal God forever places the national unit in its proper relation to the rest of the world. Realization through the national unit is only part of the great pattern that is to be formed through worldwide realization, each nation serving in its own way the One God, the Creator of the Universe, the Father of all mankind. Serving God, the national unit is a constituent member of that all-embracing and ultimate unity – humanity.

God in History

As the individual does not live alone, neither does a people. For this reason, as long as the "holy people" remains the "one people" in history, its deed – at its very best – may be only relatively effective. Its success or failure depends on the international constellation within which that people lives and strives for its goal. A people with a purpose of its own, even though this purpose be an essentially universal one, may find itself in a situation of conflict with other peoples who are guided by exclusively self-regarding considerations. Indeed, the *raison d'être* of a God-centered nation would of necessity clash with the life motifs of a universe of self-centered nations. The conflict, at times, is unavoidable and has tragic consequences for the "one people." In the history of Israel these consequences are responsible for the Exile; they have created the wandering Jew.

In one sense, *galut* is quite natural a phenomenon. For millennia, the way of life of the "one people" has been at cross-purposes with the way of life of the rest of the world. Israel could easily have come to terms with Assyria and Rome, with Mohammed and, even, Torquemada, as well as with most of its other enemies, if only it had been willing to surrender its own distinctive purpose in history. Because in moments of ultimate trial Israel was not prepared to betray its destiny as the people of God, waves of hatred and destruction have swept over it unceasingly.

Galut is not an accident, but the natural lot of the people of God. Jewish history is inseparable from world history. The intensity of the *galut* is the measure of the world's opposition to the aspirations of the God-centered people. It is the negative version of Jewish universalism. Israel is always as homeless in this world as the purpose of God with man is in exile in history. The *galut* of Israel is one of the manifestations of the *galut haShekhina,* of the exile of the Divine Presence, from the affairs of men. It is true that in a mood of rigorous self-criticism Israel uttered the words: "Because of our sins we have been exiled from our land." This is, indeed, valid when the Jewish people faces God. Facing the world, however, the truth has been formulated in the phrase: "For Your sake we constantly face death" (Ps. 44:23). From the very outset of its history Israel knew that exile would be inseparable from loyalty to its God-oriented course.[1]

The nature of Israel's exile, the intensity of Jewish homelessness, has always been the measuring rod for the moral and spiritual maturing of the world around the Jew. The wanderings of the Jewish people through lands and times are the most revealing records of the ethical and religious history of the non-Jewish world. As was the case with their first *galut* in Egypt, so most of the following exiles of the children of Israel were not God-ordained punishments but man-imposed persecutions. The question has, of course, been asked by Jews and Gentiles alike – if the immeasurable burden of suffering which is the exile is indeed undeserved, how does God allow it to happen? Why does He not protect the innocent? Why does He not intervene in time and strike down the would-be persecutor before he is able to perpetrate his ghastly crimes?

Such questions assume that a certain form of intervention in the course of history would be proper for the Almighty. Now, if such divine intervention on behalf of the innocent were the observable rule in history, then indeed the suffering of Israel through the ages would prove something. Actually, the suffering of the materially weak and guiltless rather seems to be the norm in history, so that the *galut* conforms to the

1. Even before the birth of the Jewish people, it was announced to the patriarch Abraham: "Know of a surety that thy seed shall be a stranger in a land that is not theirs" (Gen. 15:3).

norm. In truth, the case of the *galut* is a specific aspect of the general problem of theodicy. However prominent and incomparable an example of undeserved suffering the *galut* may be, it is not the only case of its kind. He who asks why God permits "the people of God" to be persecuted might as well ask why God allows any injustice to be inflicted on any of His children or creatures. Why does God tolerate any suffering of the innocent in His creation? Such questions are, of course, at the heart of the book of Job, and as old as recorded history.

The problem of theodicy, of God's justice, exists in two forms. For the purposes of our discussion I shall call them the cosmic and the historical-ethical problems. There is evil, or imperfection, which seems to be "congenital" to creation itself. This is the cosmic aspect of the problem of theodicy and I have discussed it elsewhere.[2] Now, however, we are concerned with evil as it is being introduced into history by conscious and created agencies, as the work of man and nations. And the question is, Why does not God prevent His creatures from spreading misery and sorrow in His creation?

In answer to the problem, it has rightly been pointed out that any specific intervention on the part of God would not only render the doing of evil impossible, it would also eliminate the foundations of all ethical action as well.[3]

In a world in which evil would be doomed to utter and manifest failure from the outset goodness could not prosper either. One cannot frighten people into goodness. In order to be good, man has to choose the good; but there is choice only where there is freedom. In order to be good, man must be free to be wicked, if he so desires; he must be permitted to choose between good and evil. Where there is no practical possibility for choosing evil successfully, there is no opportunity for espousing the good either. The goodness of man consists in his free commitment to the good. When I discussed the cosmic phase of the

2. Berkovits, *God, Man and History*, 100–16.
3. See Wilhelm Windelband, *A History of Philosophy*, trans. James H. Tufts (New York: Macmillan Company, 1898), 195–97, for the discussion of the problem by the Stoics. See also the discussion of the same subject in the little volume by Sallustius, translated by Gilbert Murray and published by him as an appendix to *Five Stages of Greek Religion* (Oxford: Clarendon Press, 1925).

problem, we found that an imperfect creation was freedom's only opportunity. But what is true of creation in this context is also valid of God's continued relation to the history of the human race. No doubt, God is sufficiently powerful to intervene every time a wrong is committed; it would, indeed, be a small matter for Him to eliminate all evil and injustice from the earth. But His *evident* intervention would destroy not only evil, but also the essence of man's humanity, i.e., his moral responsibility. Man is man if he may choose between alternative courses of action and if he can do so in moral freedom.

One may also put it this way: Why ask for continuous miracles to rectify matters that go wrong in the world? Would it not be simpler to ask for the creation of a perfect man, who would be so endowed by nature as to be incapable of committing any evil? The answer, of course, is even simpler than the question is naive. A perfect man is, in this sense, a contradiction in terms; it is an impossibility. A man incapable of doing wrong would not be human. The imperfection of human nature is inseparable from its most significant asset, its potential for goodness, its ability for responsible decision and action. Creating man as a morally responsible being, God had to grant him the opportunity for ethical action. The action itself must remain man's own choice or else its ethical quality is lost.[4] Man must be able to go wrong if he is to go right at all – such is the perpetual risk inherent in the human situation. The possibility of man-caused sorrow and suffering, undeservedly imposed on human beings, is always present in history – as long as man, in God's unfathomable wisdom, is permitted to seek his own fulfillment.

We may now approach once again the problem of the measureless injustice which is implied in the long centuries of Israel's exile. *Galut,* as we saw, is the outcome of an unavoidable conflict between the historic function of the "one people" and the historic ambitions of the other nations. As such, *galut* is a symptom that mankind-building reconciliation is still lacking in the world. The subhuman excesses of hatred and cruelty to which Israel has been exposed, almost without a respite, are themselves the measure of the impotence of the spirit and of the blind

4. A characteristic saying of Rabbi Ḥanina (Berakhot 33b) is that "everything is in the power of Heaven, except the fear of Heaven."

fury of the self-centered passions of man's biophysical inheritance. They bear convincing witness to the tragic truth that humanity is still only a potentiality and far from being a reality; that the deed of transformation, rendering the spiritual vital and the vital spiritually purposeful, the mitzva, has still not become effective in history. And yet, God may not manifestly intervene. History is man's responsibility. The task is man's, for only man can build mankind. Only man can overcome the dualism within himself; only if he does it himself is it overcome. Of course, God is omnipotent. If he wished to, He could miraculously destroy the tyrant or the guilty nation. But would such an act of God create interhuman reconciliation? Would it establish mankind? Certainly, it would create fear and no nation would dare lift up the sword against another and, thus, all history would be ended by universal trembling. In every miracle history is at a standstill. But the stuff of history is the deed of man. Responsibility and purpose in history have been entrusted into the hands of man.

Far be it from us to suggest that what has been said on God's silence in history is the solution to the problem of theodicy. It is, however, an important step forward to understand that the problem is not just due to human ignorance but is implanted in the scheme of things. If divine providence would indeed be manifest in the world, if it – as it were – came up convincingly to human expectations, if God acted always as man's sense of justice would want Him to, the overwhelming burden of the proof that "sin does not pay" would extinguish man's freedom to commit himself to one or the other of possible courses of action. There would be only "goodness" left, imposed from without. Man would cease being a morally responsible creature. The problem of God's providence and justice must forever remain unsolved in history, so that history itself may be possible as the process of life's increasing God-orientation through human responsibility.

Once again we may point to the concept of the hiding God, which was variously discussed in the first part of this work.[5] We saw that the

5. Kant could not accept the idea that an ethical law should have to emanate from the will of the Supreme Being. He believed that such a law could not be considered ethical – nor would the resulting fulfillment of duty be an expression of "free virtue" – but

original religious experience of the encounter had to be momentary in order to be endured by man; and even while lasting, the Divine Presence could reveal itself from behind some protective barrier, or else man could not have survived the "terror" of the Almighty. We also heard that the encounters had to be extremely rare in history, in order to leave room for doubting and, thus, to safeguard man's spiritual freedom, which is the most noble quality of faith. God is hiding from man most of the time so that man may believe in Him without compulsion. I also noted the religious need for the impossibility of proving God's existence intellectually. Any such inescapable proof would put the human intellect itself in chains, prejudicing its search for truth. Finally, we have found a fourth meaning of the concept of the hiding God in man's ethical need for the insoluble problem of theodicy. For the sake of man, God cannot *evidently* interfere in the course of history, for such intervention would completely crush man's moral independence and responsibility. The prophet said of Him: "His love leads Him to be silent" (Zeph. 3:17). The very silence of God in history is due to His concern with man.

Does it then mean that God has left His creation completely to its own devices, allowing things to take their course as they may? Such a thought would be incompatible with the responsibility of which the Creator cannot, in any imaginable way, divest Himself. Things need not happen in accordance with human insight and expectation, yet there is an ultimate responsibility which is God's. By creating man as a being

---

compulsory and legalistic. See Kant's *Die Religion Innerhalb der Grenzen* (Konigsberg, 1793), Stück 3. Kant was right in insisting that freedom cannot be separated from ethical action. Any action performed under duress could not be ethical. At the same time, however, an ethical principle must be obligatory and obligation derives from a commanding will. Kant assumed that only "*das moralische Gefühl*" and "practical reason" may provide an ethical law in freedom. The truth is, as I have shown, that they allow too much freedom and reduce ethics to complete subjectivity. For us, the will of God is the source of absolute objectivity of the ethical law. The necessary element of freedom is safeguarded by the "hiding" of God. While the desire of God constitutes the law, it is so conveyed to man that most of the time man is free to refuse to acknowledge the manifestation of God's will.

in need of spiritual, intellectual, and ethical freedom in order to fulfill himself, God took a chance with His creature. In respecting man's God-given – though limited – independence, the Creator incurs a risk with him. Man is responsible to the extent to which he is free; God is responsible to the extent to which He has made man free and sustains him in freedom. For this reason alone it is inconceivable that God departed from His creation and that He is indifferent to what man does with his life and the world.

The encounter as such, as well as the revealed law of God, are of course in themselves direct indications of the Creator's interest. At the same time, the need for divine silence in history excludes only manifest intervention; it does not eliminate indirect intervention by the Almighty. Such indirect and, therefore, not altogether convincing intervention in the affairs of men, which the human being is free to recognize or to reject, may well be one of the ways in which God discharges His responsibility by His creation. It may be a counterbalance to the risk of freedom which is inherent in life and history. For all we know, God may even intervene in the disguise of natural events, happening in accordance with natural laws. Many are His invisible or unrecognized messengers.[6]

It is not inconceivable, however, that as a result of human action, performed in freedom, or of the interplay of natural forces – and at times because of a combination of the two – a situation may arise in which divine intervention may have to be direct and manifest to all. When, for instance, the proposed outcome of history is in utter jeopardy – not to mention other imaginable possibilities – the evident act of God may be quite in keeping with what is dictated by God's own responsibility. In such cases we speak of miracles. The miracle may be one of God's ways to safeguard the intended ultimate outcome. As the human deed is a manifestation of human responsibility met in freedom, similarly – on an incomparably higher level – the miracle is an expression of divine freedom made use of in the service of divine responsibility. At times, when the deed fails, the miracle may be the only corrective. This, of course, means that miracles are not the ideal way of influencing the destinies

6. About such indirect intervention in order to punish an evildoer, who cannot be brought to justice, see, for instance, Makkot 10b, Sanhedrin 37b, and Ketubot 30b.

of men. Only the deed is according to plan; the miracle is a stopgap in history. Not only is history – as we have observed – at a standstill in the miracle; the miracle is a sign of a serious breakdown in history. The need for the miracle stems from the measure of freedom which is inherent in creation. When freedom, misused, threatens to break through the limits of the calculated risk that God took with His creation, the freedom of the Almighty may have to bring its trespassings to a halt. It is, of course, not for man to say when a situation has arisen that has to be salvaged by a miracle. Let it be sufficient for us to be able to make peace with the idea that there is, indeed, a place for the miracle within the natural scheme of things.

The question may, however, be expected at this stage: while the logical and ethical necessity for the miracle may be conceded, is not the materialization of a miracle to be considered a practical impossibility? If the question means to imply that miracles are impossible because they are contrary to the laws of nature, we must regard it as completely devoid of meaning. We need not enter here into a discussion of the numerous religious and philosophical rationalizations of the miracle which, rather than interpret the concept, explain it away. The English deist, David Hume, was perfectly right when, in defining the miracle, he maintained that the determining factor was not that an event occurred contrary to the observable laws of nature, but that it happened as the result of a direct intervention by God.[7] Putting it this way implies that not all miracles need be observable as such. At the same time, Hume's definition does say that miracles are contrary to nature. For anything to happen as the result of direct divine intervention is not natural. A miracle is indeed in its essence – even though not always in appearance – unnatural. Nevertheless, it is a poor contribution to the discussion to maintain that on this account alone a miracle could not happen. What is contrary to nature is, of course, *naturally* impossible. No one who is prepared to give credence to the possibility of miracles ever denied it. In fact, it is the point of the affirmation that the naturally impossible may happen as the result of divine intervention. The real issue, therefore, is not whether what is contrary to natural law is within the realm of natural possibility;

7. See David Hume, *Concerning Human Understanding* (1748), sec. 10, n. 21.

but whether a form of direct intervention on the part of God – as constituted by a miracle – is conceivable or not.

Obviously, the possibility of such intervention cannot be denied on the basis of God's lack of power. Starting with the premise of an Almighty Creator, it does not seem logical to deny God the might to act within His creation. As long as we consider nature a thing apart from God, as we indeed do when we see it as creation, not even a strictly deterministic interpretation of its laws will rule out the possibility of the miracle. That nothing within nature may disrupt the chain of cause and effect does not prove that the Lord of Nature may not do it. We ought to understand the philosophical significance of a position that rejects any form of direct divine intervention. There is, indeed, no way of establishing the *practical* impossibility of the miracle. The miracle may only be rejected for logical reasons as being incompatible with the premises of certain forms of metaphysics.

Such logical rejection follows, for instance, from the position of pantheism. Assuming, for example, the stoic contention that the laws of nature are identical with the laws of reason, or with those of a universal pneuma that is the soul of the universe, no intervention by God in the flow of events is conceivable. Such intervention would indicate that the laws of universal reason were faulty somewhere and in need of correction. Quite within the stoic tradition, Spinoza wrote: "for whatsoever is contrary to nature is also contrary to reason, and whatsoever is contrary to reason is absurd, and, *ipso facto,* to be rejected."[8] With Spinoza, of course, the cosmos becomes completely absorbed in God. The identification is so complete that nature disappears as a separate entity. There is only the infinite substance which is deity. Starting with such concepts, Spinoza must conclude that "the power and efficiency of nature are in themselves the Divine power and efficiency." The laws of nature are themselves the will of God; they are His decrees, "following from the necessity and perfection of the Divine nature."[9] Miracles,

8. R. H. M. Elwes, *The Chief Works of Benedict de Spinoza,* vol. 1 (London: George Bell and Sons, 1883), 92.
9. Ibid., 83.

therefore, would be contrary not only to the laws of nature but also to divine nature itself!

There is also, however, a form of theistic metaphysics from which the rejection of the miracle follows as a logical necessity. Assuming that creation was perfect, representing a divine order in completion, the need for a miracle would reveal a flaw somewhere in what was originally planned to be without blemish. The corrective measure of the miracle would indicate that a "slip-up" occurred in the divine order. It would be no less absurd to entertain such a possibility on the basis of the premises outlined than, as we heard, was the assumption according to Spinoza that anything contrary to reason could ever occur in nature.

The Spinozistic argument against the miracle need not detain us much longer. Spinoza's reasoning is cogent, but only as long as we grant his acosmic pantheism. The very essence of religion is the confrontation between man and God.[10] The religious experience of the encounter, as well as the concept of creation, are diametrically opposed to any form of pantheism. Far from agreeing with Spinoza's dictum that "the power and efficiency of nature are in themselves the Divine power and efficiency," we could only conceive of creation as an act of divine self-denial and self-limitation. Nature, as creation, is apart from God; it is outside Him, it "the other" to Him. The laws of nature may, indeed, be called the decrees of the Creator, but not as pantheism understands them as being identical with the divine will. The laws of nature are not divine but natural, i.e., created. There is no logical contradiction between such a concept of natural laws and the possibility of divine intervention in them. What is more, we have found that creation as such must be conceived as being of necessity imperfect.[11] Now, in a perfect universe – if such a one were thinkable – a miracle could never happen; all intervention with perfection can only be destructive and not corrective. Nor would there be any need for the miracle in such an order. It was in the very imperfection of the creation that we discovered both the challenge for man, and the source of his freedom to meet the challenge. Within perfection there is no choice, no alternative, no freedom. The imperfection of creation is

10. See Berkovits, *God, Man and History*, 14–15.
11. See ibid., 75–78.

man's opportunity. This same opportunity granted to man in the form of freedom and responsibility may in history necessitate the corrective act of the miracle. As the element of imperfection is the chance of human freedom, how much more may it serve as the thin end of the wedge for divine intervention.[12]

While the miracle may be the divine corrective, man's destiny on earth can only be fulfilled by man himself. The task and the responsibility are his. A man made good by a miracle is not a good man but a good puppet. The essence of goodness, as we saw, is expressed in an attitude or action consciously espoused by man and without outside compulsion. If the creation of mankind consists, as I have argued, in the achievement

12. It is, indeed, not impossible to interpret the "laws" of nature as nature's God-granted independence from the Creator. Through the laws, God might have put His creation on its feet, as it were, enabling it to go its own way to some extent. Without such laws all creation would be in continuous danger of falling apart because of its perpetual chaos and God would have the task of continually recreating the cosmos. All order would be due to the direct intervention of God; all would be miracle and utter dependence. "God created," however, means that He posited something outside Himself; He gave His creation an identity of its own; He let it be itself. Even nature can only be itself if it possesses its identity with some measure of freedom. The "laws" of nature, for all we know, may be a manifestation of such identity; they may be an indication of the course that nature chose for itself. Since God protects and preserves man's identity in moral freedom and responsibility, why could not the relationship between God and His entire creation be a similar one? To outside observation the "laws" may appear as a chain of necessity – speaking still in terms of classical physics; looked at from "within," however, they may be expressions of nature's impulses, urges, and desires in the midst of limited areas of "freedom" and "choice." Nature itself may possess some spontaneity and be capable of doing right or else of committing blunders. Whatever "freedom" and "independence" there might be within nature, it would have to be limited by divine responsibility for the act of creation. While God, in granting a separate identity to the world, took a risk with His works, the risk – nevertheless – would have to be a calculated one. As human freedom may often result in man-caused suffering, so may – perhaps – nature's freedom too at times lead to nature-caused suffering of the innocent and pure. And as in history so in nature too, the Creator's ultimate responsibility may occasionally require divine intervention.

of universal reconciliation, it can only be accomplished by man himself. Unless reconciliation is an actual experience brought about by human desire, unless it means fellowship fostered by man through his own exertions, it cannot exist. And even the day of which the prophet says: "Then the Lord shall be King over all the earth; on that day the Lord shall be One and His name One" (Zech. 14:9), cannot be the Lord's doing alone, without reference to man's success or failure in history. If it were altogether the work of the Lord, it would have been more logical to dispense with all history from the very beginning and start with the day on which "the Lord shall be King." There is a share of human responsibility in making the Lord King over all the earth by placing all life under His sovereignty. The striving for this goal is the meaning of history.

Man's redemption is, therefore, within the scope of human responsibility. That is how God willed it. While mankind, established through the self-redemption of man, is always far-removed in the future, in history one may discern its emerging outlines in the interdependence of all human destinies. No one lives in "splendid isolation"; all have their neighbors and whatever anyone does, or leaves undone, affects others and through others, in some measure, all. These facts indicate the common responsibility of the race of men. That, because of the interdependence of all life, the righteous do suffer because of the consequences of the deeds of the wicked reflects the reality of mankind in its negative state. That we are tied to each other from the beginning is the indication that we should join each other in the end. Universal redemption is the common responsibility of all.

Is it still necessary to affirm that I do not suggest that man is all on his own? He who knows of the encounter and the revelation of the law is sure of God's concern and care, with which history as man's creation of mankind is initiated. He also knows that even in the long stretches of human life during which God seemingly leaves man without a message, "His love leads Him to be silent" (Zeph. 3:17). With the boldness of faith, man may often recognize the hints for the workings of the hiding God, not to mention those rare moments of grace when man is overwhelmed by more convincing signs of divine concern. The Rabbis in the Talmud (Shabbat 119b) were right in looking on man as a "partner" of God in the works of creation. Who dare say where the share of God comes to an end and where the human contribution begins! Man may be "like nothing before You," yet God desires his "partnership."

The goal of human history may never be achieved, the unity of mankind may never become a complete reality, the day on which "the Lord will be King over all the earth" may yet have to be brought about by a culminating act of divine grace and love; but man's own responsibility never ceases, for his opportunity to strive to bring the goal closer to realization is never dead. As long as man lives, his failure cannot be final. After every failure, not only can he be forgiven but he may even start anew, if he "returns." After every failure, *teshuva* allows man to continue as if the failure had been a success. The return to God is an act of complete transformation of character. In the act of *teshuva* the past is not undone – which would be impossible – but redone. The impact of past failures becomes creative in its effect on future desire and action. The man who returns to God incorporates even his past sins in the structure of his reborn personality. Man is forever invited to return.[13] Universal reconciliation may never be achieved by man alone. Because of *teshuva*, the hope for redemption is never forfeited.[14]

What, however, is the promise that man will make use of the gift of *teshuva*; that, after his numerous and tragic failures, he will seek the way of return to God; that, in a fit of universal folly and criminality, he may not extinguish life itself from the face of the earth and thus commit his final blunder? In a sense, the question has already been answered by what was said earlier. God, in endowing man with a measure of freedom – the source of all human follies as well as achievements – accepted the responsibility for the final outcome. God alone, who called the Beginning, will call the End. God, having granted man the freedom to fail, will not let him fall irrevocably. The divine responsibility for the creation is the guarantee that the purpose of man's

13. According to the Midrash, Exodus Rabba 19:4, "The gates are open all the time and everyone who wishes to enter may do so."
14. It is noteworthy that the teachers of the Midrash interpreted the words of Kohelet, "that which is crooked cannot be made straight," by saying: it applies only to the world to come, in which one reaps the rewards of one's conduct in the present world. But as long as man lives on earth the crooked may well be made straight, for none of his actions is final. There is always the possibility of *teshuva*. See Ecclesiastes Rabba 1.

formation in freedom and for responsibility will not be ultimately thwarted. That is the root of the messianic faith. God's intention for man, as revealed in the encounter and by His law, will be fulfilled. It is the messianic promise, inseparable from history. But only the goal is preordained; the road to it, however, must be blazed by man and the time it will take to reach it depends on man. What Rabbi Yehuda said of Israel applies to the entire race: They will not be redeemed unless they return (Yoma 86b). Since in the final reckoning God will not be defeated, there is always time to return. And so we have ample failure in ample time, which means – ample suffering. The hope of man is that, through suffering, he will return to be redeemed. But redeemed he will be, for God lives.

The assurance of the messianic fulfillment of history is beyond any doubt. The most convincing indication of its coming is the survival of Israel. The survival of Judaism and of the Jewish people in all ages, in conditions of utter political and material weakness, in spite of continuous discrimination and persecution, and in defiance of an endless series of the most barbarous and sadistic attempts at their extermination, baffles all explanations. It is the mystery of all ages. The return of Israel to its ancient homeland in our days, as Israel maintained for numberless generations that it would do, is the incomparable historic event of all times. As a manifestation of the interdependence of all life, Israel's suffering is the measure of man's failure to become "a partner" with God in the task of human salvation. Israel is always as close to martyrdom as the human race is removed from being humanity yet. On the other hand, Israel's survival is by itself proof that God's purpose in history will not be defeated and, therefore, the day of mankind's reconciliation will yet dawn.

Whether the price which must be paid in terms of suffering and misery will be well worth the achievement is not within the ken of man either to affirm or to deny. Judged from the point of experience, the teachers of the Talmud have said: "It would have been better for man (the individual) not to be created"; yet, they accepted life as a task and a responsibility, for they continued: "However, now that he has been created, let him look to his deeds" (*Pirkei DeRabbi Eliezer* 43:1). Only one who knows of the original intention that moved God in creating may judge the road as well as the goal. We may have some inkling of God's purpose for man, as revealed to man by God; we know nothing of God's purpose with His creation for God. Being placed in this world, man has been invited to accept, and to cooperate with, what God desires for him. Let this suffice him.

Indeed, before the day of fulfillment and universal salvation arrives, many will have suffered because of the sins of others, many will have fallen by the wayside. What of them? What of the numberless millions who pay the price for the risk that God has taken with creation but themselves never live to see the day of justification? One can answer only by saying that our concept of divine justice demands that on the day of universal fulfillment they too must be vindicated and justified individually, just as they suffered individually. Divine justice, which is one of the ways in which we have conceived God's care for man, is the postulate of immortality. It requires that in the act of final redemption all generations that ever were born be redeemed (Eiruvin 13b). Even the dead must live to share in the realization of the promise that alone justifies the travail of all times.[15]

God, as He has made Himself known to man, is a caring God. God is our surety that nothing that has value, in accordance with His desire for man, ever perishes. He is the Preserver. Because He is, we

---

15. This should not be confused with Kant's postulate of immortality. All Kant's postulates derive from requirements of "practical reason." Since the human soul is never able to achieve the highest good in time, there must be timeless existence for the soul to achieve it, which is immortality. Similarly, since bliss (*Glückseligkeit*) is a form of harmony between the moral state of man and the state of physical nature, there must be a cause outside nature that implants the possibility of such harmony in advance. This cause is the Supreme Being. These postulates are subject to all the criticism which is rightly leveled against every form of ontology. "Practical reason" demands that the soul should be able to acquire the highest good, but this does not justify the expectation that the soul ever will acquire it; the possibility of *Glückseligkeit* asks for the positing of a Supreme Being as the originator of the moral and the physical nature, but this need not necessarily mean that such a Being does exist; it may as well be that *Glückseligkeit* is not to be achieved. The postulates that I employ do not emanate from a principle of reason, but from the reality of God's existence. The existence of God, and the nature of His relationship to man and the world, being given, the postulate of immortality follows of necessity.

know that no good deed and no kind word, no noble thought and no sincere striving for the good, are ever in vain. Because He is God nothing worth preserving is ever so lost in history as not to be found again – be it even beyond history.

Identity Problems in the State of Israel

Recently, the identity problem of the Israeli came again to my attention in two rather paradoxical yet similar manifestations. A friend of ours and her husband, both products of leftist and utterly antireligious kibbutzim, were in the United States for a limited period of continued professional education. In a recent letter, referring to Pesaḥ, she wrote:

> The Festival was for us an exciting experience. We saw the movie *Holocaust*. That introduced us into the atmosphere of Judaism. Passover we celebrated with a Jewish family. Then came Independence Day [of Israel] and we marched together with other Jews. We realized for the first time that we are part of a great people and so is the State of Israel.

The same ignorance of Judaism, the same estrangement from everything Jewish, a similar discovery of the unknown Jewish people, are all revealed in the words of an Israeli writer in an interview that was published in the supplement of the daily newspaper *Haaretz* on May 12, 1978. Speaking of his own life and that of his generation, he said, among other things:

> We were not Jews, but Israelis. The word "Jew" was hardly ever heard. We were courageous, Sabras, different. When one of us traveled to a foreign land, he would come back, saying proudly: "They didn't notice at all that I was a Jew."

For this man, the meeting with other Jews was the most severe trauma of his entire life. Where did he meet the other Jews? Not in Israel. But meeting some of the Jewish children in Europe who survived the Holocaust caused him to realize that he was, indeed, a Jew. What kind of Jew? "The truth is," says he, "that I cannot say what this Jewish identity of mine is."

The paradox, of course, is that Israelis have to leave Israel in order to discover that they are Jews. But what kind of Jews and why? Mostly, they themselves do not know. There is, indeed, a severe identity crisis in Israel, so severe that a majority of Israelis are not even aware of the "existential vacuum" (to use Frankl's terminology) in which they live. This identity problem of Israel is, unfortunately, the direct outcome of a basic mistake of modern Zionism – "normalization." The cause of the traumatic experience which overcame that Israeli author when he was "meeting with Jews," remnants of European Jewry, was probably due to the fact that for the first time in his life he realized that, after all, we are not a normal people. There was a collapse of the dreamworld in which he had lived as an Israeli non-Jew.

To become a normal people was the goal which meant, of course, to become like all the other nations. This involved, first of all, looking at ourselves from without, i.e., judging ourselves, Judaism, and Jewish history by values assimilated from alien cultures. Characteristic of this kind of self-judgment with alien eyes is the rather well-known (in Israel) short story by the distinguished Israeli writer Haim Hazaz, "HaDerasha" (The Homily), in which a young man delivers a kind of secular sermon. The gist of his homily is that the Jews have no history. They have been, most of the time, objects of history. Their history is that of the nations in the midst of which they have lived. Their history has been made for them by others; it is imposed upon them. It is all passivity. And, thus, one reaches the conclusion that the Jews are not really a nation. Only now, in the State of Israel, are they made into a nation.

All of this is true if one looks at the Jewish people from without; if one judges the Jews by a concept of history taken from others. One looks at the history of the nations and concludes: "That is not us." Indeed, it is not us. But is there, because of that, no Jewish history? Is it, indeed, all passively endowed history prescribed by others for the Jew? The truth is that, throughout the exile of the Jewish people, there were always options available to the Jew. It was already noted by Yehuda HaLevi in his *Kuzari* (the end of part 1). In the lands of their exiles all that Jews had to do in order to join the ruling majority was to repeat a few words, the creeds of the various churches, and thus become Christians or Muslims, as the case might be. At the cost of incalculable self-sacrificial commitment to the truth of their own being they rejected these options and made their choice in supreme freedom of spirit and will. If Ahad Ha'am made the comment on the assimilated Jew of the Enlightenment period that he lived in subjection in the midst of freedom, one may say of the Jewish people prior to that period that, on the whole, they lived in independence in the midst of subjection. It was a form of self-affirmation, of authenticity of being, without comparison in the history of the nations.

The argument also runs: The Jews had no country of their own, no government, no armies; ergo, they were no nation. Again, this is true if one looks at us from without. But what do we find within? Scattered all over the world, the Jews were one. Except for minor local variations, they all lived by the same values, pursued the same lifestyle. Wherever Jews met, they encountered each other in mutual recognition. Notwithstanding language differences, they all prayed in the same tongue, according to the same order and, essentially, the same prayers; observed the same holy days; observed the same laws. The literature of the various communities was Jewish literature for all. The talmudic as well as philosophical works written in any one community were meant for all communities. They had no government, yet they governed themselves. For centuries Jews lived by an internal autonomy. The rabbinical courts were a generally recognized and effective judiciary. The communities were guided only by elected committees. The *takkanot hakahal,* communal ordinances, were the laws that prescribed order in all matters affecting the material as well as the spiritual-religious well-being of the communities.

Whereas in the rest of the world general education for all social levels of the people was introduced relatively late, the institution of general education was in existence in all the lands of Jewish exile and had an uninterrupted tradition going back to talmudic times. In all of the communities there were, for the poor and the sick, welfare services whose historic continuity paralleled that of the educational system. All of this internal autonomy was maintained without state power; it required no police enforcement. On the whole, it functioned by the moral force of a self-imposed discipline, unique in the entire history of the human race.

Certainly, there was Jewish history of the Jew's making, but a different one.

Certainly, we are a people, though unlike the other nations. Not a normal people? Looking at the history of the "normal" nations one need not be embarrassed by the qualification.

Zionism's striving for "normalization" meant a misreading of Jewish history. Thus, it destroyed the Jew's self-understanding. Secondly, "normalization," knowingly or unknowingly, implied the rejection of Judaism and required the reshaping of the Jewish people in an alien image. But this precisely is impossible. A nation may grow, develop, renew itself from its own resources of the mind and the spirit, in a continuous process of loyalty to its own identity. But a people that refuses to understand itself from within, that cuts itself loose from the meaning of its historic course, that has no respect for its historic identity, is bound to fail. National identities cannot be exchanged; neither can a people turn its back on its past and start from scratch. There are no such beginnings in history. The image, therefore, in which this people was to be reshaped was essentially a negative one, a shattering of the historic molds.

Israel was built with rebellion. This was, in a sense, necessary, and worked well for the founding generation. The giants of that generation were all children of the Judaism of the ages against which they rebelled. Y. H. Brenner testified about himself that in his youth he had a thousand double pages of the Talmud in his head. The same Brenner would also write: "I live in shame as I recall God's loving-kindness that keeps me alive every minute and that yet I rebel against Him."[1] His writings are rich with biblical and talmudical phraseology and thought associations. That was a generation that had its identity roots completely in historic Judaism. The emotional quality of its being came from the shtetl; the pattern of its intellectual expressions had been largely determined in the *beit midrash*. That founding generation came because they returned to the land of their fathers. Thus, A. D. Gordon would write of the situation in the land:

> We all agree that our position is dangerous. Our fate hangs by a hair between life and death. Yet, we are unwilling to confess to ourselves that our salvation will come only from a giant, almost miraculous effort of the will, so that in a certain sense we may say, together with the masses of the people, that we shall be redeemed and saved for eternal salvation only by way of a miracle.[2]

This rendering into English is somewhat awkward because Gordon uses classical Jewish messianic terminology. The power of the faith that moved him and his contemporaries was essentially a manifestation of the force of Jewish messianic belief in return, an authentic transformation of that belief in a new context, in a new historic situation.

Notwithstanding their rebellion, their values had their origin in the "old home," though they were applied in a new context and, thus, often became enriched. Let us recall here Gordon's idea of nationhood. He writes:

> The nation as a "collective individual" is a tearing animal. There is not another one like it for cruelty and meanness among all the wild beasts of prey. Acting as a nation, it is not only permitted to tear, to kill, to rob, to steal, to lie, to forge, to defile, to commit

1. Y. H. Brenner, *Kol Kitvei*, vol. 1 (Tel Aviv: Dvir, 1964), 26.
2. Aharon David Gordon, *Mekhtavim UReshimot* (Tel Aviv: Histadrut HaTziyonut, 1957), 32–33.

> all kinds of abominations, but such acts redound to the nation's fame and glory, for which it is worthwhile sacrificing one's life.[3]

That is what Gordon sees as history and nationhood, whose absence among Jews is so deeply regretted by Hazaz's hero in "HaDerasha." When we read Gordon, we immediately feel the passion of the Jew behind his words. His ideal is, what he calls, Am-Adam, a phrase one can render only awkwardly as "Nation-Man." Behind his Hebrew Adam one hears its Yiddish equivalent, Mensh, not just in the sense of a human being, but a humane human being. Am-Adam is a humane nation. Gordon also puts it this way:

> Where there is no humane nation, there will be no humane human, no humane individual either. And who should more insist on this than we, the children of Israel! We were the first to declare that man was created in the image of God. We have to go further and say: The nation has to be made in the image of God. Not because we are better than the others; but because everything [in human experience] that demands it we have endured and suffered on our own shoulders.[4]

There is no "normalization" here, but complete identification with all Jewish history. There is also here a going further and beyond the Old Word. But what is spoken is the Old-New Word of Judaism.

All this was rebellion within the continuity of Jewish history. It was an internal, Jewish rebellion, carried out with an inherited idealistic fervor. But, alas, all this is no longer. The rebellion of the founding generation is long past. The Sabra may well live in existential frustration, but he is not a rebel. He has nothing to rebel against. It is worth noting how Berl Katzenelson, one of the outstanding leaders of the early labor movement, who was also the founder of the Histadrut, expressed his misgivings regarding the future. These are his words:

---

3. Aharon David Gordon, *HaUma VeHaAvoda* (Tel-Aviv: Histadrut HaTziyonut, 1952), 260.
4. Ibid., 160.

> That one generation should rebel against another is natural. That, however, one generation should tear itself loose from another, which then becomes like one that never existed, is a special curse from our *tokheḥa* (the portion in the Bible that describes the punishment that will befall the Jewish people for not keeping the Torah)... A generation that does not know its father, does not know itself; it does not know what it has inherited and against what it rebels.[5]

Unfortunately, the present generation in Israel does not only not know the "father" of whom Katzenelson spoke, who is its "grandfather"; it does not even know its own fathers, i.e., Katzenelson, Brenner, Gordon, and others in the same category. The founders, who – in spite of their rebellion – were heirs, did not succeed in becoming ancestors. This was succinctly expressed by one of the *vatikim* (a veteran; in this case, a kibbutznik of the old generation), whose words were quoted in an article in the literary publication of the kibbutzim (communal settlements, mainly secular and – often – antireligious), *Shdemot*. Speaking of his son, the man remarked: "He is not a Jew. I wished he were, at least, a socialist."[6]

This son is no exception, not even in the kibbutzim. Outside of them, in the cities, such souls are much more numerous. Nature does not tolerate a vacuum; much less does the life of a people. The spiritual and value vacuum caused by a Zionism without Judaism has been filled by a crude Levantinism and a vulgar imitation of the cheapest forms of American materialism. In the earlier days of Zionism one was apprehensive of the dangers of national assimilation. One has now learned to understand that only a minority may become meaningfully assimilated. There is a great deal that is objectionable in contemporary America. But a minority has the option to assimilate itself to what is positive and noble in the American tradition and civilization. The same is true of any minority in the midst of any other historic culture and tradition. Not so a majority that lives in its own land. It has nothing to which to assimilate itself. It must be itself; it must live by its own spiritual resources

5. See *Kitvei Berl Katzenelson*, vol. 7 (Tel Aviv: Mapai, 1944), 163.
6. Yariv Ben-Aharon, "Open Criticism, Open Love," *Shdemot* 6 (1976): 92.

lest it become the inheritor of the cultural refuse that, in these days of easy worldwide communication, reaches its undiscerning and uncritical populace in large and intense doses from the international conglomerate of disintegrating value systems.

In the aftermath of the Yom Kippur War there has been, in limited circles, some awakening to the nature of the problem. Questions have been asked: "Why Israel and for what?" If one is an Israeli outside of the historic continuity of the Jewish people and of Judaism, a people without a past, without Jewish ideals, cut off from anchorage in the historic culture and tradition of Judaism, separated from the source of its creativity, then, indeed, what is Israel for? Why the never-ending struggle, the wars, the internal as well as external problems, the eternal tension of a little country under continuous siege? Under these circumstances, nothing is more natural than the large emigration of Sabras in search of greener and quieter pastures. What is more difficult to understand is why so many of them, assuming that they do have the opportunity to leave, remain: Is it some form of macabre blood-and-soil nationalism?

Some mean to meet the problem by what they call a "return to the sources." What they actually engage in is a form of literary activity of looking for universalistic, humanitarian "gems" in the Midrash and Talmud. I doubt very much that this kind of literature can fill the place of a people's lack of faith in its historic destiny. The news that the old-time rabbis were not always old-fashioned will provide neither goal nor direction for the Israeli masses, and certainly not a disciplined will and commitment to pursue a new and different course of value-determined behavior. Ideas are not ideals and for "quotations" to be effective one needs foundations.

The Israeli author, to whose interview I referenced at the beginning of this essay, also declared: "Yes, I seek my Jewish identity. However, I cannot find it here." In the context of the interview he was saying that the search for his Jewish identity among the Jews in the United States, where he had spent some time previously, was much more promising than in Israel. Here, of course, is the acme of the paradox. Unfortunately, from the Israeli vantage point, it is not altogether unjustified.

This takes us to the other aspect of Israel's identity problem, the religious sector in Israel. Needless to say, the majority of religious Jews, rather like the majority of the secular ones, are hardly aware that such a problem exists for them, too. Who can be more sure of his Jewishness than an Orthodox Jew living in the Holy Land of his fathers! The question is, however: Is this, indeed, the Jewish identity that the Torah intended for the Jew living in a Jewish state? Is this, indeed, the Judaism required by the Torah for the Jewish people in its regained homeland? In view of the abysmal ignorance about what Judaism really is, the majority of Israelis see Judaism in the image in which it is presented to them by the rabbinate, the heads of the yeshivot, the religious establishment. One may be extremely critical of Israeli secularism, as obviously this writer is, and yet realize – with an aching heart – that this rabbinate, these teachers of the Torah, these guardians seldom command one's respect. On the whole but for a very few exceptions, they are incapable of conveying the meaning and relevance of Judaism to the people in the context of this completely new reality of statehood.

The image that is thus presented makes it easy for the secularist intellectual to produce his "straw man," call it religion or Judaism, and knock him down with a great deal of self-assurance, using the outworn arguments of a nineteenth- or even eighteenth-century "enlightenment." The image that is presented is essentially that of *galut* Judaism and of the *galut* Jew. It is so unimpressive because it is placed in the altogether wrong setting. *Galut* Judaism, as the only possible form of Judaism in the *galut,* has its validity. Transferred to the condition of Jewish statehood it becomes inauthentic. In order to explain our meaning it will be necessary to recall some of the essential qualities of classical Judaism.

Religions are usually founded by prophets; Judaism was founded by a father. At the beginning of Judaism stand patriarchs; the prophets teach in historic realization what was intended by the fathers. Abraham did not establish a church; his concern was not with the salvation of souls. He was a father, concerned with the life of his children. God says of him: "For I have chosen him so that he may direct his children and his household after him to keep the way of the Lord by doing what is right and just" (Gen. 18:19). A family whose ideal was to observe the way of God, to act justly and righteously, became the Jewish people. Judaism is not a salvationist religion, but the way of life of a people, lived with the realization that all life is forever in the presence of God. God is the eternal witness. The words of the psalmist: "I shall walk in the Lord's presence in the land of the living" (Ps. 116:9) are explained by Rabbi Yehuda: "'The land of the living,' i.e., the marketplaces" (Yoma 71a). It is in the midst of life that Judaism is to be realized.

The task to live with the awareness that all life is in the Divine Presence is all-comprehensive. It includes man's relationship to God as well as to his fellow men. It is not only a matter of creed, but essentially one of deed. It has its ramification in all the fields of human existence: spiritual as well as material, social and political, economic and cultural. It was not to be limited to a church or a religious sect, but had to become the life purpose of a people. Only a people might be capable of such a comprehensive realization of an all-embracing life purpose. Therefore, the normal, natural habitat of Judaism is a land of the Jews, Eretz Yisrael. Outside of Eretz Yisrael, in all the habitation of the Jews, the structure of society, of public life, the social, economic, and political order are determined by cultures and civilizations that are not Jewish, that are alien, and often inimical to Judaism.

Thus, wide areas of Jewish teaching, especially as they found their formulation in halakha, in Jewish law, have no possibility of application. For instance, wide sections of the *Ḥoshen Mishpat,* dealing with the judiciary, with civil and criminal law, or important parts of the *Even HaEzer,* containing family law, husband and wife relationships, remain a mere subject of study, a matter of theory, without any practical application. Judaism is then reduced, halakhically, to a code of *mutar* and *asur,* a regimen of the permitted or the forbidden. It was meant to be the essence of the realization of the life purpose of the Jewish people. In the Dispersion, not only the Jewish people but Judaism, too, is in *galut.*

Congregations, synagogues, temples can realize the goal only fractionally – services, observances, the family, the Jewish child – but life in its comprehensive fullness is not their domain. Only the people, in control of its own national existence, is capable of realizing the inclusive life purpose of Judaism.

The Rabbis taught: "There is no Torah like the Torah of Eretz Yisrael" (Genesis Rabba 16:4). But why so? If it is Torah, it is Torah everywhere; if it is not, it is not Torah anywhere. How is the quality of Torah understanding tied to geography? If the quality of Torah understanding depended only on study, geography would not matter. However, Torah understanding is inseparable from the range of Torah application. In the *galut,* Torah application is limited essentially to the *reshut hayaḥid,* the private domain, the individual, the home, the congregation. Only very little room is left to Torah in the *reshut harabbim,* the public domain. We may better appreciate the importance of the fullness of Torah application to actual life situations as we recall that the halakha, that is the discipline of such application, was originally *Torah Shebe'al Peh,* Oral Torah. Rabbi Yosef Albo, in his *Sefer HaIkkarim* (3:23), explains the need for the "Oral Teaching" in the following manner:

> It is impossible that the Torah of God, blessed be He, be complete in such a way that it should be adequate for all times. For the particulars that are changing in the affairs of men, in judgments and matters affected, are too many to be contained in a book. For this reason Moses, on Sinai, received, orally, general principles that are concisely hinted at in the Torah, so that with their help the teachers of each generation may reach their decisions regarding those new particulars.

Halakha was meant to deal with specific life situations. But that situation is forever changing. The new, the unexpected in the human condition, is the raw material with which halakha has to contend. It looks at the situation, it considers the basic principles and then decides. Now, the situation in the *galut* is essentially non-Jewish; it is brought about by the changes and developments in the midst of a non-Jewish reality. When, then, halakha is asked to speak its word in a new situation that had not previously existed, an unfair burden is placed on the halakhic potential. The question put to it is: How to order Jewish life in the midst of changing non-Jewish situations? It can be done. And it has been done for many generations with determination, heroism, and sacrifice. But it is not the natural function of halakha to teach this.

It is, for example, the natural function of halakha to teach the observance of the Sabbath in all kinds of changing human situations. But the Torah was given to the Jewish people with a view to their living in Eretz Yisrael, with the power to determine the rhythm of the working week. It is, of course, possible – and Judaism considers it an obligation that has been accepted by the Jewish people for its entire history – to observe the Sabbath even in the *galut*, but that is not the natural setting for the Sabbath. Problems of Sabbath in Exile, for instance, how to make a living in the midst of an economic order that rests on Sunday, are not genuine Sabbath observance problems, but part of the much wider issue: how to be a Jew in the not-originally-intended and unnatural setting of Jewish dispersion. The original function of the halakha is, thus, adulterated, when it is forced to contend with the everchanging "particulars" of a non-Jewish reality in the midst of which Jews happen to live.

As a result, halakha is negatively affected in two directions. It cannot shape and guide the specific time-conditioned situation, and it must defend itself, it must defend Jewish existence, against the pressure and inroads of the "outside world." In the *galut*, halakha becomes a rampart and yet, as the word itself indicates, it was intended to be a pathway. In the *galut*, halakha is Torah managing Jewish existence in spite of the nature of a form of life and culture that is alien to the spirit of Judaism. Halakha on the defensive becomes stunted in its creative capacity. This has far-reaching consequences for its very nature. Halakha as the application of the general principles to the ever-new particulars, once again to use Albo's formulation, needs the challenge of those "particulars," the challenge emanating from the contemporary situation of the Jewish people. It needs the challenge of a situation that is Jewish, not because it is endured by Jews but, in its physical and mundane structure, is the work of the Jewish people. That, alone, is the authentic challenge to halakha. Only in response to this challenge, in this confrontation, can halakha become creative, formulating the eternal word of the Torah for the new hour, the hour of the new "particulars."

All this, of course, is possible only in a Jewish state. This is the meaning of the uniqueness of *Torat Eretz Yisrael*, of the Torah of the Land of Israel. In the State of Israel, Albo's "new particulars" are Jewish. They are Jewish raw material for halakha to work with. The *galut* attitude of defense is no longer valid. One has to go out and meet this new challenge and show how this new Jewish reality is to be structured meaningfully and effectively by the creative power of halakha. One has to leave the ramparts built around the "private domain" of the congregation, the Jewish school, or the home in *galut* and restore halakha to its original function as a pathway for the "public domain," for the life of the Jewish people in a Jewish state. To mention just a few areas: halakha in the State of Israel ought to concern itself with the social gap, with questions of economic honesty and fairness, with issues of the work ethos and problems of labor relations, with medical ethics, even with such matters as meaningful driving laws in the cities and on the highways and with adequate enforcement.

How far removed we are from a proper understanding of what Torah and halakha are about cannot be more strikingly illustrated than by the one-sided educational ideal of the yeshivot in Israel. Most of them frown on what is called *limudei ḥol*, secular learning. But a state needs an army, an economic system, health and welfare services, technology, scientific research, etc., etc. If the Torah desires a Jewish people living in its own land, it must also desire soldiers, physicians, scientists, architects, engineers, policemen, social workers, etc., etc. In a Jewish state, halakha cannot refuse responsibility for the effective functioning of the entire body politic. This requires, however, a new educational philosophy, which would lead, in turn, to new ways of learning Torah and Talmud and new ways of teaching both.

The new reality of the State of Israel demands an understanding of what halakha is about in its original, classical essence. Perhaps one of the major issues to which such new understanding ought to pay attention is the fact that in a state of Jews one is not dealing with congregations but with a people. It is relatively easy to manage the congregational structure. Congregations have their declared ideologies. Those who subscribe to them are in, those who do not are outside. One may lament the attitude to the outsiders, but one need not be concerned about them very much. A people, however, is always within. Halakha, in its authentic function, must address itself to the Jewish people and not to members with congregational ideologies. What we have in Israel today is a *galut*-conditioned understanding of halakha and its application to a *galut* reality that was, but is no longer. It is the halakha of the shtetl, not the halakha of the state; it is not *Torat Eretz Yisrael.*

It is this that robs teachers and interpreters of convincing authority and respect. In the shtetl they were part of the community, deeply involved in its life and problems. In Israel they live in estrangement from this new reality of the Jewish people. The psychological effects of such alienation are often responsible for a behavior that is deeply regretted by many Jews to whom the dignity of Judaism is dear.

There is widespread secularism in Israel today. But there is also an awakening to the truth that, especially in Israel, secularism is leading the people into a spiritual and moral dead-end street. There are many who search for a Jewish way. The people will not be the Jewish people and the state not a Jewish state without Judaism, and Judaism will not be true to itself without finding the way to the people.

Alienation from Judaism is the source of the "existential vacuum" among the secularists. Alienation from the new reality of Israel's statehood renders questionable the authenticity of the image of Judaism that has been transferred from the *galut* by the religious establishment. And yet, this is the land and this the people. It is here, in the land of Israel, that the destiny of all Israel will be decided for all generations to come. Thus, the problems of this land become the problems of the entire Jewish people the world over. Their solution is the responsibility of us all.

The fonts used in this book are from the Arno family

Other books in the **Maggid Modern Classics** series

When God is Near
Rabbi Yehuda Amital

Faith after the Holocaust
Rabbi Eliezer Berkovits

Ḥadarav: His Inner Chambers (forthcoming)
Rabbi Abraham Isaac Hakohen Kook

Orot
Rabbi Abraham Isaac Hakohen Kook

By His Light
Rabbi Aharon Lichtenstein

Return and Renewal
Rabbi Aharon Lichtenstein

Values in Halakha
Rabbi Aharon Lichtenstein

Pathways to God (forthcoming)
Rabbi Nachum L. Rabinovitch

Pathways to Their Hearts
Rabbi Nachum L. Rabinovitch

Faith Shattered and Restored
Rabbi Shagar

Living Time (forthcoming)
Rabbi Shagar

Confrontation and Other Essays
Rabbi Joseph B. Soloveitchik

Halakhic Morality
Rabbi Joseph B. Soloveitchik

On Repentance
Rabbi Joseph B. Soloveitchik

The Lonely Man of Faith
Rabbi Joseph B. Soloveitchik

Perpetuating the Masorah
Rabbi Yitzhak Twersky

Maggid Books
The best of contemporary Jewish thought from
Koren Publishers Jerusalem Ltd.